Ancient Near East

A Captivating Guide to Ancient Civilizations of the Middle East, Including Regions Such as Mesopotamia, Ancient Iran, Egypt, Anatolia, and the Levant

Free Bonus from Captivating History (Available for a Limited time)

Hi History Lovers!

Now you have a chance to join our exclusive history list so you can get your first history ebook for free as well as discounts and a potential to get more history books for free! Simply visit the link below to join.

Captivatinghistory.com/ebook

Also, make sure to follow us on Facebook, Twitter and Youtube by searching for Captivating History.

Contents

INTRODUCTION 1

CHAPTER 1 – MESOPOTAMIA: THE BIRTH OF THE FIRST
CIVILIZATION..3

    SARGON: THE EMPEROR AMONG KINGS...4

    THE RISE OF AN EMPIRE AND THE BATTLING CITIES OF SUMER.......................7

    THE CHILDREN OF SARGON THE GREAT AND THE FALL OF THE AKKADIAN
    EMPIRE 10

    CULTURE, GOVERNMENT, AND MILITARY OF THE AKKADIAN EMPIRE 13

CHAPTER 2 –EGYPT: THE UNIFICATION OF UPPER AND LOWER
EGYPT AND THE BIRTH OF THE PHARAOHS 16

    NARMER: THE FOUNDER OF THE FIRST DYNASTY AND THE PHARAOH OF A
    UNITED EGYPT 20

    THE RISE AND FALL OF THE FIRST DYNASTY IN EGYPT 21

CHAPTER 3 – ANCIENT IRAN: FROM EARLY URBAN SETTLEMENTS
TO THE RISE OF THE ELAMITES..26

    THE EMERGING ELAMITE CULTURE 27

    THE THREE RULING DYNASTIES OF THE OLD ELAMITE PERIOD.................... 29

    CULTURE, GOVERNMENT, AND MILITARY OF ELAM 34

CHAPTER 4 – ANATOLIA: THE BRIDGE BETWEEN ASIA AND EUROPE
AND THE RISE OF THE HITTITE OLD KINGDOM 37

    THE RISE OF THE HITTITES IN ANCIENT ANATOLIA 39

CHAPTER 5 - THE LEVANT: THE KINGDOM OF EBLA AND THE CULTURES OF THE ANCIENT LEVANT 45

THE RISE AND FALL OF EBLA AND OTHER ANCIENT SYRIAN KINGDOMS 46

CULTURE, MILITARY, AND GOVERNMENT OF EBLA 51

CHAPTER 6 - THE RISE OF THE ASSYRIAN EMPIRE AND BABYLON FROM THE ASHES OF AKKAD 54

THE THIRD DYNASTY OF UR 56

THE RISE OF BABYLON AND THE FIRST AMORITE DYNASTY 59

CULTURE, GOVERNMENT, AND MILITARY OF THE ASSYRIAN EMPIRE 62

CULTURE, GOVERNMENT, AND MILITARY IN HAMMURABI'S BABYLON 63

CHAPTER 7 - THE OLD AND NEW KINGDOM OF EGYPT: DYNASTIC EGYPT AND THE RISE OF POWER IN THE BANKS OF NILE 65

THE RISE OF THE EIGHTEENTH DYNASTY AND THE NEW KINGDOM OF EGYPT: THE EGYPTIAN EMPIRE 76

MONOTHEISM IN EGYPT WITH PHARAOH AKHENATEN AND QUEEN NEFERTITI 78

THE RULE OF TUTANKHAMUN AND THE END OF AMARNA 80

THE PEAK AND END OF THE NEW KINGDOM - THE WARRIOR KINGS 81

CULTURE, GOVERNMENT, AND MILITARY OF EGYPT 84

CHAPTER 8 - THE MIDDLE AND NEW KINGDOMS OF THE HITTITE: THE DARK AGES AND THE GLORY OF THE HITTITE EMPIRE 87

THE LEGACY OF TUDHALIYA I: THE NEW KINGDOM AND THE RISE OF THE HITTITE EMPIRE 89

HATTUSILI III THE WAR KING AND THE DEMISE OF THE HITTITE EMPIRE ... 93

CULTURE, MILITARY, AND GOVERNMENT OF THE HITTITE KINGDOM 96

CHAPTER 9 -BEYOND THE WARS AND THRONES: THE EVERYDAY LIFE OF COMMON PEOPLE IN THE ANCIENT NEAR EAST 98

EVERYDAY LIFE IN MESOPOTAMIA 98

EVERYDAY LIFE IN ANCIENT EGYPT 100

EVERYDAY LIFE IN THE HITTITE KINGDOM 102

EVERYDAY LIFE IN HAMMURABI'S BABYLON 103

CHAPTER 10 - THE BIRTH OF RELIGIONS IN THE ANCIENT NEAR EAST: THE CRADLE OF CIVILIZATION AND THE GODS 106

RELIGIONS IN MESOPOTAMIA 107

RELIGIONS IN ANCIENT IRAN 107

RELIGIONS IN ANATOLIA 108

RELIGIONS IN THE LEVANT 109

RELIGIONS OF EGYPT 110

CHAPTER 11 – POLITICS AND INTERNATIONAL RELATIONS IN THE
FERTILE CRESCENT 112

CONCLUSION 115

HERE'S ANOTHER BOOK BY CAPTIVATING HISTORY THAT YOU
MIGHT BE INTERESTED IN 117

FREE BONUS FROM CAPTIVATING HISTORY (AVAILABLE FOR A
LIMITED TIME) 118

REFERENCES 119

Introduction

Where did the first signs of civilization appear in the ancient world? When did people start to transition from the nomadic life of hunters and gatherers to living in the first urbanized settlements? Who was the first emperor in history? Which empire was the strongest and mightiest, and for how long? Where did the title "King of the Universe" come from, and who was the "True King?" All these answers are hidden in the ancient history of the Fertile Crescent, and now, they are unveiled to you in our comprehensive and captivating guide to the ancient civilizations of the Near East.

Take a journey back in time and meet the first emperor and the mysterious legend that surrounds his origins. Find out who was the first pharaoh to unite the kingdom of Egypt, and discover the time when a woman ruled ancient Mesopotamia. You will also find out about the first people to inhabit the Levant and Anatolia, as well as how Persia lost their hegemony in the Levant. Join us as we discover the power of agriculture, trading, writing, and commerce, to the rise and fall of the first major empires in the world.

Between myths and facts, one can discover an ancient world that set the first stone to the foundation of civilization. The beautiful Near East, the cradle of different ethnicities, nationalities, legends, and religions, has slowly been unveiling its ancient secrets, and in these pages, you can travel the hallways of time to uncover a distant past that gave life to society as we know it.

Chapter 1 – Mesopotamia: The Birth of the First Civilization

We are going back to the late 4th millennium BCE to get to know the oldest literate civilization: the Sumerians in Mesopotamia. Sumer encompassed the southernmost part of the great civilization of Mesopotamia, where southern Iraq now lies. Mesopotamia itself covered a vast region, and it included the modern-day territories of Iraq, Kuwait, Syria, and Turkey. Interestingly, the name of Sumer means "the land of civilized kings." Based by the river system of the Tigris and Euphrates, this powerful civilization rose to become the home of some of the most powerful empires over the centuries to come. One such empire was ruled by the Akkadian dynasty.

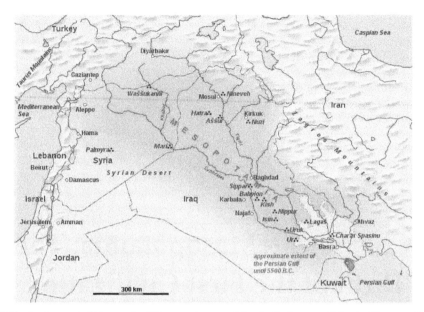

Washukanni, Nineveh, Hatra, Assur, Nuzi, Palmyra, Mari, Sippar, Ba bylon, Kish, Nippu, Isin, Lagash, Uruk, Charax Spasinu, and Ur, from north to south.

(https://images.app.goo.gl/q4vFcNZT4ng1Qact6)

Numerous positive factors affected the rise of the first civilization in Mesopotamia. For one, the area was practically booming in life when it came to agriculture. Where one can find fertile soil and a favorable climate, there is food, and where there is food, there is always most certainly life. And this time, it was not just any form of life—it was civilized life. To grow a true civilization, the Sumerians had to do more than farm and irrigate successfully. They invested in magnificent architecture, promoted literacy, and had a sophisticated military system.

Sargon: The Emperor among Kings

According to the scriptures and legends dating from the late 4th millennium BCE and even centuries later, Sargon wasn't the first ruler of Mesopotamia and the Fertile Crescent. However, Sargon of Akkad became the first ideal model of a ruler, and he created the first empire known in the history of civilized men. The dynasty of Akkad is known to have commenced with Sargon of Akkad, who was once a cupbearer for Ur-Zababa, the second king of the Fourth Dynasty of Kish, who ruled around 2334 BCE.

Before Sargon rose up to transform the Fertile Crescent into an empire, a feat that had been unseen in the ancient world, dynasties oversaw Mesopotamia, which the people considered to be sacred. And it all began with one man: Alulim. According to the ancient scriptures found in the area and the mythological portion of the Sumerian King List, Alulim was the first king of Mesopotamia, and he ruled over Eridu, a city in southern Mesopotamia, sometime before 2900 BCE. Sumerians believed the gods themselves appointed the rulers, as the kingship is said to have descended from the heavens. Ancient scriptures created by the Sumerians thousands of years ago even list a king that supposedly lived and ruled in Mesopotamia for over 48,000 years. And supposedly, women ruled Kish as well. According to the Sumerian King List, a woman named Kubaba ruled from around 2500 to 2330 BCE. It is very unlikely she ruled for this long, but it is believed that she was the grandmother to none other than Ur-Zababa.

Ur-Zababa, like other rulers before him, resided in the city of Kish, which was located in today's territory of Tell al-Uhaymir. Ur-Zababa and the Kish dynasty was defeated by the king of Uruk in around 2375 BCE. Uruk was another ancient city of Sumer; it was located east of the present-day Euphrates River. Lugal-zage-si, who was originally the king of Umma, another ancient Sumerian city, was the leader behind this attack. He was perhaps the first king to come near the title of emperor before Sargon of Akkad appeared on the scene. Besides Kish and Uruk, Lugal-zage-si is said to have conquered other Sumerian cities, such as Lagash, with his main goal being to form a unified kingdom of Mesopotamia. According to the Sumerian List of Kings, Lugal-zage-si, who ruled Kish for twenty-five years, was overthrown by Sargon of Akkad.

It is hard to differentiate between fact and the whimsical legends that surround the life and deeds of Sargon of Akkad. Even Sargon's origins are veiled in myth, but the Sumerian King List states that he was the son of a farmer and the king's cupbearer.

But why would a king choose a modest farmer's son to serve him as a cupbearer? To answer the question, historians can only turn to the ancient scripture known as *The Legend of Sargon*. The legend is actually Sargon's autobiography, which is why it must be analyzed with reserved accuracy. Sargon weaved an interesting story to justify his right to the throne. He particularly wanted to present his rule in an appealing light to the commoners, who were suffering from famine at the time due to unflattering political conditions.

Sargon appeared to be very much aware of the demographics he ruled over as emperor and the times he lived in. He belonged to both worlds after his conquest—the world of commoners and the world of kings—but yet, he was neither. He was an emperor. Sargon made sure to emphasize his modest origins instead of hiding the fact that he was the son of a farmer. However, Sargon added fantastic details to his origin story that made him into a half-god—a man in the favor of the goddess Inanna. His autobiography states that he was born to a changeling priestess serving in the temple of Inanna, which gives him a connection to the divine, something that all kings searched for to prove their legitimacy to rule. Although historians can't claim with complete certainty what the word "changeling" means in *The Legend of Sargon*, it is thought that "changeling" refers to the temple priestesses who worshipped Inanna, as they were androgynous. Since Sargon was illegitimately brought into this world by a priestess who couldn't keep him, Sargon says he was placed in a basket and set upon the currents of the Euphrates River. According to the legend Sargon wrote himself, he was found by a modest farmer, who took care of him as if Sargon was his own flesh and blood. The man who found Sargon in a tar-sealed basket was named Akki, and he was a farmer or a gardener in the service of King Ur-Zababa, who ruled the

Sumerian city of Kish. If Akki was a gardener, he most likely would have taken care of the royal gardens, as this would explain how Sargon came in contact with King Ur-Zababa and became his cupbearer.

The scripture considered to be Sargon's "autobiography" was written long after the first emperor was gone; however, historians believe the written version represents Sargon's own story of his modest upbringing and birth under strange circumstances. Sargon wanted the people to see a poor boy, a castaway who had made it against the kings and the elite to do what no one else before him could—build an empire and unite all of Mesopotamia under a single ruler. In reality, historians can confirm that there are not many clear pieces of evidence that reveal the true origin of Sargon. The very fact that Sargon wasn't his real name helps to show this. Sargon was a cleverly minted name that means "True King."

Regardless of his true origins, Sargon successfully formed the first multi-national empire and also formed a new line of monarchs known as the Akkadian dynasty. To this day, no opposing version of Sargon's origins has emerged, which is why Sargon is still presented as an orphaned son of a priestess. Sargon is the first known ruler to have conquered all of Mesopotamia, although this feat would take him some time. The first emperor was to be remembered as Sargon the Great, the first of his name, "king of Akkad, overseer of Inanna, king of Kish, anointed of Anu, king of the land, governor of Enlil."

The Rise of an Empire and the Battling Cities of Sumer

Even though it may not appear so, Lugal-zage-si cleared the path for Sargon to become the first emperor of Mesopotamia. Before Lugal-zage-si's conquest, Sumerian cities were frequently at war, battling over territory and the water supply. Lugal-zage-si managed to unify the cities of Sumer; however, his kingdom was still an incohesive union. Lugal-zage-si made his own glory by becoming the first king of Sumer to succeed in conquering the majority of Sumerian city-states; he is also remembered as the last king before the rise of the Akkadian Empire. After conquering Uruk, he decided to try his luck with Kish. Upon hearing Lugal-zage-si's plans, Ur-Zababa decided to offer a treaty. According to *The Legend of Sargon*, Ur-Zababa had a dream where he was told that Sargon would be his end. So, the king decided to send Sargon to take the treaty to Lugal-zage-si, asking the conqueror to kill Sargon after he read the message. For some unknown reason, Lugal-zage-si decided not to kill Sargon but instead offered him an alliance. Sargon joined Lugal-zage-si, and together, they defeated and subdued Kish. In the chaos, Ur-Zababa escaped and went into hiding. There are numerous legends revolving around Sargon, so it is not clear what happened afterward. What is known is that Sargon and Lugal-zage-si soon came to be enemies. Some sources indicate that Sargon was banished by King Lugal-zage-si for having an affair with the queen. Sargon decided to take Uruk by matching into the city, after which Lugal-zage-si challenged him in the city of Kish, a challenge he lost. After capturing Lugal-zage-si, Sargon made him march in chains to acknowledge his own demise. Sargon then proclaimed himself the king of Kish and continued to conquer the rest of Sumer.

In addition to warfare and conquests, Sargon also had to face internal conflicts. The reason Sargon most likely decided to place emphasis on his modest origins was the steaming political situation between the elite and poor laborers. Of course, the poor laborers outnumbered the rich and powerful. Sargon's politics and the image he created of himself, in combination with his unquestionable talent in military skills, appealed to the oppressed Sumerian society. It is crucial to note that very few people at the time lived in abundance and prosperity. The wealthy, who controlled the cities of Mesopotamia, were only becoming wealthier, while the poor were suffering, with no chances to acquire a more prosperous life. Long days of work with little to show for it created discontent among the poor. When Sargon took over the leadership, this discontent seemed to settle somewhat. By conquering the entire region and subduing all the Mesopotamian city-states, Sargon could equally dispense the collected riches across his new empire, which could help resolve the discontent caused by famine to some extent. Sargon also created a centralized authority in Mesopotamia with effective administration that employed people he trusted across different regions and cities.

The path toward building the first empire wasn't easy, but the image Sargon presented to the poor and rich alike granted the emperor the hegemony he needed in the southern parts of Mesopotamia. However, Sargon's political ideals and claim to the throne didn't appeal to everyone. Sargon described numerous revolts he needed to deal with before he was able to create a cohesive empire.

After defeating Lugal-zage-si and conquering Kish, Sargon established a new capital—Akkad, also known as Agade—by the banks of the Euphrates River. He wasn't satisfied with ruling a small territory, and with the Sumerian elite challenging his right to the throne, Sargon decided to continue with war campaigns. He had support from the military, as Sargon himself was described as an exceptional military leader. He decided to cross the Tigris River and take the Elamite lands, in which he succeeded. He didn't stop there, for he decided to take his campaigns north and conquer Mari. Sargon went pushed even deeper to demonstrate his power in the land of the Amorites, west of the Caspian Sea. Ashur and Nineveh were next in line, which were farther to the north, and Sargon campaigned in Asia Minor as well. Every march and every campaign only helped Sargon grow his empire. It is entirely possible that he even conquered Cyprus and enabled trade with India, which would make his growing empire even richer.

Sargon conquered one city after another, and any ruler who didn't recognize him as the new king was soon forced to accept him as the ultimate ruler. One of the reasons Sargon's military campaigns were so successful is that he created the first institutionalized military practices, which made his army more adaptable and mobile.

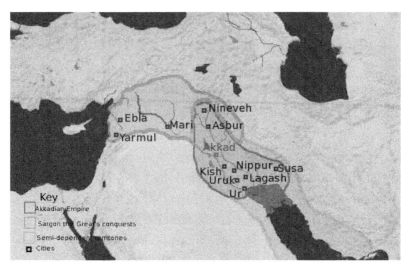

Sargon the Great's conquests: Ebla, Yarmul, Mari, Nineveh, Asbur, Akkad, Nippur, Susa, Lagash, Kish, Uruk, and Ur
(https://images.app.goo.gl/ZLWikBCfVkCvAKbg6)

Sargon was equally capable of leading an empire. He ended up ruling over sixty-five cities. Sargon wanted to make sure that the administration would reaffirm his rulership, so he employed sixty-five governors to lead these cities on his behalf.

The Children of Sargon the Great and the Fall of the Akkadian Empire

Sargon the Great conquered sixty-five cities of the Fertile Crescent in thirty-four battles. Those who wouldn't kneel before him were soon forced to, as Sargon managed to unite all the cities of Mesopotamia, including the people of Sumer and Akkad, under his rule. It is hard to know when Sargon accomplished the following feats, as the chronology of his rule only covers the first five years; after this point, it is just descriptions of his conquests. Sargon attacked the land of Subartu and conquered the tribes of Kazallu, decimating the land so badly that there was nothing left. All of the regions that bordered the Akkadian Empire became vassals to Sargon. Two millennia after his death, Sargon would be held up as a model ruler across the Semitic empires, as he was the first ruler of a multi-ethnic empire, who acquired the right to the throne with his might and military skill.

Near the end of his rule, Sargon was faced with famine and wars. The revolts that Sargon successfully silenced in the early days of his empire were slowly starting to rise again. Sargon was already around fifty-five years old by this point, and he was presumably too weak to protect his empire. Sargon was besieged in the capital of Akkad around 2286 BCE; however, the emperor was an exceptional military leader, which helped him achieve a victory when he decided to battle against the members of the revolt.

Sargon had three children: a daughter, who became a priestess serving the goddess Inanna, and two sons. The throne was inherited by his first son, Rimush, in around 2279 BCE. It is perhaps needless to say that he and all his successors were more or less in the shadow of Sargon, who had even created the title "King of Everything," also interpreted as "King of the Universe." The title was used by Mesopotamian kings who reigned long after Sargon's death.

Rimush was immediately faced with revolts by the cities his father had previously conquered. Rimush was forced to reclaim the cities of Umma, Der, Lagash, Kazallu, Ur, and Adab from the rebels. The cause of Rimush's death remains unknown, as he didn't die in any of the battles he conducted against the rebelling cities, nor did he fall during his victorious campaigns against Barakhshe and Elam. It is presumed that Sargon's first successor died by the hands of his own courtiers. Regardless, Rimush only ruled for nine years before his brother took over.

Manishtushu, Rimush's brother, inherited the throne around 2270 BCE. His rule would last for fifteen years. There were few to no rebellions during the rule of Manishtushu, so the king focused on campaigns in the Persian Gulf, south of the Akkadian Empire, and the cities along the Tigris River. His son would take over the rule after Manishtushu died in c. 2255 BCE.

Manishtushu's son, Naram-Sin, would bring the empire to the peak of its glory. Naram-Sin justified the name of his grandfather's dynasty and created the title "King of Four Quarters"; he also carried the title forged by his grandfather, "King of Everything." Naram-Sin translates to "Beloved by the Moon God," and he was the first ruler of Mesopotamia to consider himself a divinity. Naram-Sin also gave himself the title of "God of Akkad." Naram-Sin conquered the regions by the Mediterranean Sea, as well as Armenia. He faced a rebellion from the city of Kish but was able to silence it with his military power. He took control over Elam and also conquered Armanum and Ebla, facilitating another golden age for the Akkadians. Naram-Sin's rule was the longest after the approximate fifty-five-year rule of his grandfather, Sargon.

The fall of the empire would become obvious during the rule of Shar-Kali-Sharri, the son of Naram-Sin. Shar-Kali-Sharri was the last king to rule the Akkadian Empire as a whole, and he came to power in circa 2217 BCE. He united all the cities of Sumer and the regions his father had conquered during his thirty-six-year rule. The Akkadian Empire started to fall apart around the time of his death in around 2193 BCE, as a severe drought occurred, which brought famine to the people. After the king's death, four potential successors—Igigi, Imi, Nanum, and Ilulu—took turns on the throne, with all four ruling for short periods of time due to the chaotic nature of the empire. Dudu took the throne in around 2189 BCE. He ruled for a longer period of time, about twenty-one years, but he was the penultimate ruler of the Akkadian dynasty. Shu-turul, his son, would inherit the throne around 2168 BCE. Little did he know that the Gutian invasion would put an end to his reign in circa 2154 BCE. The famine made it easier for the Gutian people to conquer the Akkadian Empire when they descended from the Zagros Mountains at the end of the 3rd millennium BCE. The Guti, who were nomadic people before their conquest of the Akkadian Empire, formed their own dynasty after overrunning southern Mesopotamia. Most of the cities in the southern area of Mesopotamia were deserted due to the severe drought at the time. However, one empire's demise meant another empire would rise. And one of the most notable empires of Mesopotamia did so: the Assyrian Empire. This empire will be covered in more depth later on. In the meantime, another civilization in the ancient Near East was developing and achieving glory on the banks of another powerful but more predictable river, that of the Nile. This civilization was none other than Egypt.

Culture, Government, and Military of the Akkadian Empire

Before the Akkadians, the city-states of Sumer didn't have a standing army. There were professional soldiers employed to protect the city, but there were no legions of soldiers with the capacity to carry on conquests like those led by Sargon. This army counted perhaps several hundred soldiers or even a thousand. It is not known whether the soldiers were paid or simply volunteered to protect the territory of Sargon's conquests. As time went by, Sargon's army became larger. After all was said and done, Sargon had an army of around 5,500 men. Sargon came up with an idea to recruit soldiers from defeated city-states after conquests, which set new standards and military traditions for empires that came later. Sargon appeared to have had a great talent in warfare, which can be testified through the invention and use of the composite bow. This bow had three times greater impact power when compared to the commonly used wooden bow. For the most, the army was composed of infantry units, but it is possible that some units included horses and chariots later on. It is not difficult to imagine how the threatened city-states viewed the first standing army ever to be seen in the history of the ancient world. Watching an army march toward the city gates with Sargon the Great at its head would bring fear to anyone's heart. It was an effective military strategy as well, as people would often surrender without a fight.

Sargon must have been a talented statesman as well, or else his newly conquered empire would have crumbled. However, he understood the need and importance of administration, as it would keep his war-won empire intact. While his empire was growing larger, he created an organized administration, where he employed people he trusted to oversee the city-states he had conquered. These people were known as *ensi*. Some of the city-states were overseen and administered by local *ensi*, while some cities were governed by Sargon's most trusted officials. This decentralized administration worked in unison with the emperor. For the first time in history, an empire with colorful cultural, political, ethnic, and religious backgrounds was founded, and these differences had to be somehow tamed and neutralized so as not to cause the demise of the Akkadian Empire.

Sargon wanted to establish a strong, unified, powerful, and rich kingdom—an ambitious endeavor that he succeeded in. Sargon realized during the process of unification that the peripheral city-states would be difficult to control under the autonomy of the Akkadian Empire. Some of these cities were located far from the center of the empire, and they varied in demographics and agricultural production. Their use was quite limited, so instead of subduing these states, Sargon used treaties. Through these treaties, the emperor was able to create a strong commercial network while also keeping the city-states under his control. His grandson and successor, Naram-Sin, built strongholds to gain better control over this trading network. One such stronghold was in Tell Brak, an ancient city-state in Syria whose original name is not known to history. It is presumed there were more strongholds built across the commercial system that Sargon created.

Civilized and organized societies in the ancient world are noted by their development of a collective identity through language and an alphabet. In the case of the Akkadians, they used the now-extinct East Semitic language known as the Akkadian language. The language used a cuneiform script, which is one of the earliest forms of writing that uses wedged marks on clay tablets. Thanks to the political and imperialistic influence of the Akkadian Empire, the Akkadian language became the common language of Mesopotamia and a great part of the ancient Near East before the end of the Bronze Age around 1200 BCE.

Chapter 2 –Egypt: The Unification of Upper and Lower Egypt and the Birth of the Pharaohs

Before the Early Bronze Age brought the Akkadian Empire to the top of the ancient world and then into oblivion, Predynastic Egypt had yet to dream of its future glory. Predynastic Egypt, also known as prehistoric Egypt, is presumed to have begun with some of the earliest human settlements in the ancient Near East. This period ended with the Early Dynastic Period, which occurred around 3100 BCE when the first pharaoh ruled over the fertile soil of the Nile. The Predynastic period is marked by numerous different civilizations and settlements that found their home around the Nile River. They would help shape the future glory of ancient Egypt. In the Neolithic period, Upper Egypt was settled by the Tasian, Badarian, and Amratian cultures. The Tasian culture flourished around 4500 BCE on the eastern bank of the Nile. It is the oldest-known culture that existed in Upper Egypt in the Predynastic period. To archaeologists, this culture is best known for its brown and red pottery, which they coated in black paint outside and inside. Archaeologists were able to keep track of the general development of the Tasian culture based on the pottery handles. Over time, the pottery handles would gradually transition from practical to ornamental. This pottery also indicates that the Badarian and Tasian cultures overlapped at one point between 4500 BCE and 4400 BCE, as the pottery found in both cultures don't have any significant differences.

The Badarian culture flourished between 4400 BCE and 4000 BCE. The Badarian sites have revealed some of the first agricultural settlements. These people were located in El-Badari, Egypt, which is about 200 kilometers (124 miles) northwest from modern-day Luxor. Their settlements revealed signs of an early civilized society based on the excavation of graves. It was discovered that the Badarian people used to bury the more prominent members of their community in separate tombs. The Badarian culture made tools such as axes, arrowheads, and hooks. Besides agriculture, they also relied on fishing and the domestication of animals for wool, milk, and meat. Their art was rather simple, usually depicting animals, such as hippopotami, and they were buried with objects such as female mortuary figures and ore amulets.

The Amratian culture, also known as the Naqada I culture, developed between 4000 BCE and 3500 BCE. The archaeological site of el-Amra, after which the Amratian culture was named, is around 120 kilometers south of Badari, Egypt. The black-topped ware found in the Tasian and Badarian cultures was still produced; however, a unique type of white-lined pottery appeared with the Amratian culture. The Amratian was also noted as the first culture in Upper Egypt to own slaves, and they used papyrus-based rowboats to sail the Nile. They started to trade goods with Lower Egypt, sending them items like vases, beads, and other similar artifacts. The Amratian people imported smaller amounts of gold and obsidian from Nubia. Other items they traded for include emery, cedar, and marble. Their deceased were occasionally buried with dogs, and each village in the settlement had its own statue protector of an animal deity.

During the period of the Gerzeh culture, also known as the Naqada II culture, which lasted from around 3500 BCE to 3200 BCE, the first brick of the foundation of dynastic Egypt was laid. The Gerzeh period in Upper Egypt coincides with the Uruk period in Mesopotamia (during the 4th millennium), which was the first time the two cultures ever met.

At this point, the Akkadian Empire had yet to rise. Before this happened, the Nile River was about to give birth to one of the strongest and most glorious civilizations of the ancient world: ancient Egypt. During the Gerzeh period, Egyptians started to farm along the Nile due to the radical decline in rainfall, although hunting was not a forgotten skill. With more advanced agriculture, food supplies started to rise, and the number of people living in the cities of Upper Egypt was increasing as well. Mud bricks, which were first found in the Amratian period, were mass-produced in Upper Egypt to meet the demand for more homes.

During the Gerzeh period, Egyptian culture was significantly influenced by Mesopotamia in the domain of art and through the exchange of letters. The two civilizations also traded goods, such as pottery, art, grain, linen, papyrus, iron, copper, timber, lapis lazuli, ebony, myrrh, and incense. The Sumerian script that originated in Mesopotamia probably influenced the development of Egyptian hieroglyphs. Although the Gerzeh culture is considered to be the most predominant in prehistoric Egypt by many Egyptologists, Naqada III, also known as the Protodynastic period, is considered to be the true introduction to the future glory of ancient Egypt. Naqada III brought about Egyptian hieroglyphs, advanced irrigation systems, and a glimpse into the first royal burial places that somewhat resembled the majestic pyramids that appeared in the Old Kingdom of Egypt.

The Protodynastic period is also known as Dynasty 0, as it was when the first concept of rulers appeared in ancient Egypt. The people of ancient Egypt now had advanced irrigation systems, copper tools for multiple purposes, weapons, and trade relations with other civilizations in the ancient Near East. This led to an ever-increasing population in the cities and the development of city-states along the banks of the Nile. The series of conquests led by the different cities in the area created three bigger city-states in Upper Egypt: Thinis, Nekhen, and Naqada. The time was ripe for someone to rule.

The first king of Egypt is veiled in mystery, as his existence can't be proven. His name was Iry-Hor. While some historians argue that Iry-Hor wasn't a king since his name was not written in a serekh—a heraldic crest that contained royal names—he is still considered to be the first Predynastic pharaoh. It is presumed that Ka succeeded Iry-Hor, although it is not known for certain who Iry-Hor's immediate successor was. Ka ruled the city of Thinis around the 32nd century BCE, and many historians believe he conquered all of Upper Egypt, thus placing this region under the ruling hand of the Thinite royal family.

Succeeding Ka, which is read as "King's Arms" or *Sekhen* ("to embrace"), was another king from the Thinite line: Narmer. Narmer is sometimes known as Menes, but historians are divided on the issue. Menes is the name given to the first king of Egypt in ancient sources. However, the coronation of pharaohs included an Egyptian tradition that bestowed a name in honor of Horus. This practice has its roots in Iry-Hor's name, which means the "Companion of Horus." If that is the case, Menes would be the name Narmer received after he was coronated with his two crowns—a red crown to signify his rule over Upper Egypt and a white one to mark his hegemony in Lower Egypt. This was the first time in the history of Egypt that this unification happened. Once Narmer took the throne, Upper Egypt invaded Lower Egypt, forming a united Egyptian kingdom. The act of unification marked the start of the First Dynasty and the beginning of a new era for Egypt.

Narmer: The Founder of the First Dynasty and the Pharaoh of a United Egypt

When Narmer took the throne, Egypt was already partially unified. Although the unification of Egypt is attributed to him, it began long before, although it was perhaps not seen as official.

After the unification, Horus became the main deity of the kingdom, which both Upper and Lower Egypt agreed upon. Lower and Upper Egypt also shared an alphabet and culture, taking on the form of a true kingdom. According to Manetho, an Egyptian priest and historian who lived in the early 3rd century BCE, Narmer ruled for sixty-two years. According to Manetho, Narmer was killed by a hippopotamus sometime in the 31st century BCE. The First Dynasty continued with Hor-Aha, who is believed to be Narmer's son, although some claim he was the real Menes.

Hor-Aha, abbreviated from Horus Aha, translates to "Horus the Fighter." By the time Hor-Aha came to the throne, his father had already improved the quality of life in the Egyptian kingdom. Narmer had introduced improvements to the everyday life of ancient Egyptians, including irrigation systems, a system of mathematics, practical and effective healthcare, roads, obelisks, and increased agricultural production. People started to use cloths to cover their tables and couches, introducing a more elegant way of life on an everyday basis. Narmer also promoted the idea of human sacrifices, which were supposed to assure company and protection for the pharaoh in the afterlife. An average Egyptian wouldn't be affected by this practice, as this tradition didn't include the mass killing of commoners. Instead, the pharaohs would take a couple of servants to accompany them in the afterlife. Hor-Aha continued that tradition. In fact, all of the pharaohs of the First Dynasty engaged in this practice; once the First Dynasty ended, so, too, did the tradition of human sacrifices. Before his death, Narmer transferred the capital of the kingdom from Thinis, where his line had begun their rule as Dynasty 0, to Memphis. As such, Memphis would be the capital of Hor-Aha.

Memphis was chosen as a capital for strategic reasons, as the only threat to Egypt would have come from across the Mediterranean. Memphis was located near modern-day Cairo to the south. That way, Egypt could see any threat arriving, which would give them time to prepare defenses. Even though Memphis was made the capital of unified Egypt, pharaohs would be buried in Abydos. Abydos plays a major role in Egyptian religion. According to Egyptian myth, Abydos was sacred to Osiris, as it was the place where Isis buried Osiris after assembling his cut-off body parts. It was also the city where Osiris was resurrected. Symbolically, pharaohs of the First Dynasty were buried in Abydos in hopes of resurrection.

To continue his father's legacy over the unified kingdom of Egypt, Hor-Aha performed many religious duties and focused on the luxuries Egypt had at the time, such as marvelous craftsmanship and abundant food.

The Rise and Fall of the First Dynasty in Egypt

Hor-Aha didn't have the ambition to continue the trading relations Narmer had developed with other civilizations in the Fertile Crescent. However, Egyptians still enjoyed a life of luxury, at least by ancient standards. Even though Hor-Aha reduced commerce between Egypt and other regions of the Crescent, such as the southern Levant, the pharaoh engaged in war campaigns. For instance, he attacked the Nubians while leading an expedition.

After the death of his father, Hor-Aha's mother possibly married one of her son's most trusted grand viziers. The king's mother, Neithhotep, is believed to have outlived her son, and she took over the throne as queen regent before her grandson, Djer, was old enough to inherit the throne as the rightful pharaoh. It is thought that Djer ruled around forty years in the mid-31st century BCE. Djer is said to have had five wives, who were all buried in tombs next to his own. Djer fathered a daughter, Merneith, and a son, Djet. After Djer died around 2980 BCE, Djet assumed the throne. At some point, Djet and Merneith married. Egyptologists believe that Djet had more than one wife, just like his father, continuing the tradition of polygamous marriage. Moreover, when Djet married his sister, the Egyptian pharaohs began another tradition, that of marrying their closest relatives to protect the bloodline. They were practicing incest for the sake of the dynasty. Before this tradition, earlier kings were known to have married their daughters and sons to other wealthy families to establish diplomatic relations with powerful families. With Egypt unified under a single pharaoh, it appears the goal was to keep the land in unison by limiting the power to one family—the royals of the First Dynasty.

Historians are not certain about the exact time of Djet's rule, although some inscriptions indicate that his reign lasted ten years. After his death, Djet's throne is presumed to have been inherited by his sister-wife, Merneith, who ruled before their son. Their son, known as Hor-Den or simply as Den, was the fourth pharaoh of the First Dynasty. He began his reign around 2970 BCE and ruled for forty-two years. During his long reign, Pharaoh Den is said to have brought prosperity to the kingdom, as well as innovation to court life. Even though his rule commenced decades after the unification of Egypt, Den was the first pharaoh of Egypt to adopt the title of "King of Lower and Upper Egypt," and he was the first to be depicted wearing the double crown colored in white and red to signify the unification of Lower and Upper Egypt, although it is believed Menes invented it.

Den is the first well-attested king of the First Dynasty, as many sources mention him. Moreover, it is thought that he was the most praised pharaoh that Egypt had seen so far. Den had many sons and daughters, but it is not known for sure if his successor, Adjib, was actually his child. The First Dynasty is more or less veiled in mystery, and there are no reliable sources that credit Adjib as being one of Den's sons. However, what is certain is that Adjib took the throne after Den.

Adjib, also known as Anedjib, Hor-Adjib, Hor-Adjib, and Enezib, ruled around 2930 BCE. The ancient Egyptian historian Manetho credits Adjib with ruling for twenty-six years, while other sources state that the king ruled for seventy-six years. However, modern Egyptologists suggest that Adjib couldn't have ruled for more than ten years, as Manetho often exaggerated the length of pharaohs' reigns. Adjib wanted to legitimize his rule over all of Egypt, so he introduced a new title to the reign of pharaohs, known as the Nebuy-title. This title was written with the representations of two falcons, and it means "the two lords," which refers to Seth and Horus. The title also symbolically indicates that the pharaoh's rule was established in Upper and Lower Egypt. What makes Adjib stand out as an ambitious king is the extraordinarily high number of cult statues he created for himself and the building of a new royal fortress. This was done to create an appealing image of the ruler for the people of Egypt. Judging by the inscriptions found in Adjib's tomb, his rule may have ended violently. Unfortunately, the cause of his death remains unknown. Historians suggest that Adjib had many children, but none of their names are known to history, except for possibly one: Semerkhet.

The name of Semerkhet's mother in the Palermo Stone—a fragment of an ancient stele, also known as the Royal Annals—is Batirset, although the name is not attested by other sources. However, since Egyptologists believe the throne was inherited within the bloodline of the First Dynasty, Semerkhet is thought to be one of the many sons Adjib had during his life. Although there are speculations that Semerkhet might have been a usurper, this theory can't be confirmed. Based on Manetho's records on Semerkhet's reign, the rule of Semerkhet started with some sort of calamity, which, judging by the records, marked his short rule as the king of Egypt. Manetho believes that the occurrence of natural disasters during his reign indicates that he was a usurper who was being punished for assuming a throne that was not rightfully his. Semerkhet was buried close to the tomb where Den was buried, suggesting that he was closer to Den than Adjib, his predecessor. Since Semerkhet is known to have removed the name of Adjib, his predecessor, from many contemporary scriptures, along with the fact that he was buried close to Den, it is presumed that Den was Semerkhet's father. That would make Adjib his brother.

Semerkhet began his rule around 2920 BCE, and he ruled for eight and a half years. His name is translated as "thoughtful friend" and "companion of the divine community," which is why some Egyptologists suggest that Semerkhet might have been a priest. He didn't use the title Adjib used—the Nebuy-title—but took the title Nebty, signifying "Two Ladies." The two ladies are most likely the goddesses Nekhbet and Wadjet. Semerkhet's full prenomen (throne name) was "he of the two ladies, the king of Upper and Lower Egypt." One of the most interesting facts about Semerkhet is that his name features a rare hieroglyph. The hieroglyph shows a man in a cloak carrying a stick, and there are many theories on what the hieroglyph could mean. The symbol could be translated as "divine guardian," "guardian of the Two Ladies," or simply "guardian." This hieroglyph depicted a ceremony that was performed by priests.

The throne was next inherited by Qa'a, also known as Ka'a. Qa'a is thought to be the last king of the First Dynasty, as a war between the First and the Second Dynasties occurred. Qa'a could have been Semerkhet's son, but according to modern-day historians, he might have been the son of Adjib. According to the scriptures and the fact that Qa'a celebrated two Sed festivals, the last pharaoh of the First Dynasty probably ruled for at least thirty-three years. The Sed festival was used to celebrate the thirty-year mark of a pharaoh, and it repeated every three to four years after the first celebration. Qa'a appears to have had a prosperous rule, but Egypt found itself engaged in a war for the throne after Qa'a passed away. Thus, the death of Qa'a also meant the death of the First Dynasty.

Around 2900 BCE, Qa'a died. After his death, a war took place, and two names appear in the fight for power over the fertile lands of Egypt: Sneferka and Horus Bird, who were two supposed royals that might have had nothing to do with the First Dynasty. These ephemeral rulers are not very well known to Egyptologists, as even the way their names are read is disputable. While some historians read the name of Horus Bird to mean "Soul of Horus," others translate it as "the Heir of Horus." In the tradition established in the First Dynasty, each pharaoh was given a Horus name with their coronation. This is why it is presumed that Horus Bird was a pharaoh, although there is not much evidence on who his parents or relatives were or for how long he ruled. Both Sneferka and Horus Bird ruled for a short period, fighting over the throne of unified Egypt with the ruling First Dynasty falling apart. Along with Horus Bord and Sneferka, another royal name appears on the list of throne successors: Hotepsekhemwy. He became the first pharaoh of the Second Dynasty of Egypt after breaking up the war between Sneferka and Horus Bird. With Hotepsekhemwy as the next pharaoh, Egypt entered a new era and welcomed a new royal line. The remains of the First Dynasty are all left in Abydos in the form of royal tombs, and they remind us of the era when Upper and Lower Egypt became one.

Chapter 3 – Ancient Iran: From Early Urban Settlements to the Rise of the Elamites

Ancient Iran is home to some of the oldest known civilizations, modestly rising alongside the development of unified Egypt and Mesopotamia. Before Mesopotamia became the first empire in the history of civilization and the greatest force in the Fertile Crescent, the territory of ancient Iran saw some of the earliest urban settlements, which date to around 7000 BCE. The oldest lowland village of southwest ancient Iran, Chogha Bonut, rose in 7200 BCE. The settlement of Chogha Bonut would become the epicenter of the Elam civilization's early development, which was one of the most dominant civilizations of the Susiana Plain.

Chogha Golan, located in the foothills of the Zagros Mountains, was one of the earliest agricultural communities, where the first signs of cultivation and the domestication of plants and wild animals have been noted to start as far back as 10,000 BCE in the Middle Paleolithic period. By this time, the communities of Iran had already started to express their cultural identity through art by creating rock sculptures and ornaments. Chogha Golan was one of the first places in the Fertile Crescent where domesticated wheat was used as a food source. The people fished and hunted red deer, pigs, sheep, and goats, along with cultivating lentil, grass pea, barley, and wheat. Over time, the community of Chogha Golan flourished, growing and developing on more than just the agricultural scale. They used grinding stones and mortars to process grains, turning their crops into some kind of rough flour. This flour might have been roasted or cooked before being used for food. They also used mudbrick walls and plaster floors for buildings.

Chogha Mish, located in western Iran, emerged in 6800 BCE, and its people thrived on the domestication of pigs and horses. They dominated the Susiana region at the time.

Early connections between the Susiana Plain and Mesopotamia can be noted in the history of Chogha Mish, more specifically in pottery found in Mesopotamia and the vicinity of Chogha Mish. Up until 4400 BCE, Chogha Mish was the area with the largest population in the Susiana Plain before Susa was established as the dominant settlement in the region. The Chogha Mish settlements showed significant developments prior to the Elamites taking over as the dominant culture. Some of the earliest kilns (chambers with thermal insulation properties used for making tiles, bricks, and pottery) were found in Chogha Mish. The appearance of literacy is also noted in the settlements, as Chogha Mish and Susa used clay tokens as an accounting system. This system transformed into clay tablets using marks, which gradually became the first model of a cuneiform writing system. The people of Chogha Mish eventually migrated, and some reestablished their villages in Susa around 4200 BCE when the city was formed.

The Emerging Elamite Culture

The Elamites appeared around 3300 BCE, first taking the area on the Iranian Plateau with its center at Anshan. The center of Elam was later shifted to Awan in the mid-2nd millennium BCE.

Map of Elam

(https://images.app.goo.gl/9ws8cH3PRP4Byw1bA)

The history of Elam at the very beginning of its development was turbulent, as the power over the state was constantly shifting between Elam and Mesopotamia. Unfortunately, it appears that the powerful hand of Mesopotamian rulers was stronger than the Elamite culture and the hunger, or the lack thereof, for a powerful unified kingdom of the Elamite people.

The records of the first king of Elam emerge in 2650 BCE. Before that period, no significant historical figure appears to have carried the role of the ruler of Elam. In 2650 BCE, according to the Sumerian King List, King Enmebaragesi of Kish took over Elam and subdued the region in the name of Sumer and the First Dynasty of Kish. Elam was once again influenced by an outside culture, assimilating with the culture of Sumer and Mesopotamia. With the conquest of Enmebaragesi, Elam entered a new era in history known as the Old Elamite period, which lasted from around 2700 BCE to 1500 BCE. Enmebaragesi was allegedly killed by Gilgamesh's predecessor, although some sources indicate that the very Gilgamesh from the Sumerian *Epic of Gilgamesh* put an end to the rule of Enmebaragesi.

During this period of Elamite history, three different dynasties are said to have ruled and protected this region. With that being said, Elam was not completely freed from the influence of Sumer in the

Old Elamite period. At the end of this era, Elam would witness a great return to its cultural origins, and a new ruling dynasty would emerge to mark a period in the history of Elam known as "Elamization."

The Three Ruling Dynasties of the Old Elamite Period

Elam was rich. The Elamites had easy access to some of the biggest shipping routes across the Persian Gulf, which is how the people of Elam had access to artwork, food, and other items from many different civilizations. When looking at their location, it is not hard to determine that the region was also agriculturally strong, which means that Elam didn't have to depend on others for food. Due to their wealth, Elam was a constant target of kings who wanted to bring the known world to its knees. After thousands of years of shifting power, the Old Elamite period, although it began with a Sumerian conquest, brought Elamite dynasties to the throne. Three different dynasties emerged amongst the Elamite royal rulers: Awan, Shimashki, and Sukkalmah.

The dynasty of Awan was the first known dynasty of Elam to be mentioned in the history of the Elamite people. This dynasty overcame rulers who were in constant conflict with Mesopotamian and Sumerian rulers. The first ruler of the Awan dynasty is sadly unknown to history. Some sources indicate the Awan dynasty took over the Elamite throne in 2350 BCE, while the Sumerian King List suggests the dynasty only had three rulers, who ruled for a combined 356 years. The length of their rule cannot be confirmed, though, so the list is most likely inaccurate, as the same source suggests that Enmebaragesi, the Sumerian king who invaded Elam, ruled for centuries.

While the Sumerian King List only mentions three kings of the Awan dynasty, a list of royals found in Susa, an important city of Elam, suggests the dynasty had twelve kings. The list even provides the names of these kings, although some parts of the names are missing.

Archaeologists agree that the list cannot be considered completely reliable due to the lack of other evidence that would support the existence of twelve Awan kings.

The Sumerian King List mentions that the Awan dynasty came to power once the first Awan king defeated the First Dynasty of Ur. Ever since its humble beginnings, Elam had always feuded with Sumer, and the very fact that Awan defeated the First Dynasty of Ur in their territory gives the dynasty great importance. Elam and Sumer may have had a love-hate relationship, but business boomed between the two. The Elamites imported all kinds of foods, and they exported wool, slaves, cattle, silver, and many other things to the city-states of Sumer. The people of Elam also had some technological advancements, which also made them great craftsmen. There is a record of a request from Sumer for the governor of Uruk, a city in Elam, to turn tin into bronze. This indicates that the Elamites might have had more advanced technology than the Sumerians at the time.

Although Elam and Sumer might have had strong trading connections, the Awan dynasty engaged in several campaigns in Mesopotamia, trying to conquer some of the most powerful city-states of Mesopotamia at the time: Lagash and Kish. On one occasion, a party of 600 Elamites tried to plunder Lagash but were successfully defeated.

The Awan dynasty continuously feuded with Mesopotamia and its city-states. These little wars go all the way back to the Akkadian Empire and the rise of Sargon. Around 2300 BCE, Sargon was involved in a series of campaigns across the Iranian Plateau. Texts have been found that testify to Sargon's glory and success in these incursions, of which plunder was a standard part. Sargon defeated the eighth king of the Awan line, Luh-Ishan, the son of Hishiprashini. The Susa list of Awan kings doesn't quite match these texts; according to that list, Hishiprashini was the ninth king. Perhaps the names of the kings were mixed up, but there might also be some names missing from the Akkadian scriptures.

Whatever the case may be, after Sargon created the perfect conditions for Elam to be conquered, his son Rimush completed this venture with the defeat of the Awan king. This series of defeats brought the western lowlands of Elam under the ruling hand of the Akkadian Empire. A peace treaty between Elam and the Akkadian Empire came into being after Sargon's grandson succeeded the throne from his father. Naram-Sin, the third king of the Akkadian dynasty, signed a peace treaty that created conditions for Elam to not be assimilated completely. Although the Akkadian dynasty might have defeated the Awan dynasty, some city-states in Elam were never reached by Akkadian troops and thus were never vassals to that great empire.

The capital of Anshan was one such city, as it was located in the steep mountains and was geographically unreachable and secluded. The Elamites were able to preserve their cultural identity, although they were not content with the way things turned out. Over time, their hatred toward the Akkadian Empire grew. The tensions would not cease until the oppressed Elamites saw the Akkadian Empire fall to the Gutian soldiers. The Elamites helped contribute to the fall of the first empire in the ancient world, as they simply waited for their moment to strike. Even though the list of Awan kings of the Susa king list isn't a reliable source of information when it comes to the kings and their names, as well as the ruling order of the Awan dynasty, it does tell us who the last Awan king was: Puzur-Inshushinak, who ruled around 2100 BCE. He is remembered as the Awan king who brought independence to the people of Elam, people who had lived far too long under the ruling hand of the Akkadian kings. However, every great empire meets its demise, and the Akkadian Empire was no exception. And when one empire falls, another one rises—and the Elamites eagerly seized their opportunity.

Puzur-Inshushinak, the last king of the Awan dynasty, carried the title of governor of Susa and military governor of Elam, which was the title carried by the governors of the Akkadian Empire. Puzur-

Inshushinak, however, called himself the "Mighty King of Elam." This was found in the inscription known as "Table au Lion," or "Table of the Lion," a monument. To achieve independence for his people, Puzur-Inshushinak headed out on a series of conquests, conquering some of the most important cities in Mesopotamia, including Akkad, Akshak, and Eshnunna. He considerably weakened the Guti as well, chipping off a good portion of their newly conquered territory. The most likely reason why Puzur-Inshushinak became one of the most remembered kings of the Awan line was his commitment to preventing the assimilation of the Elamites by the Mesopotamians. He was dedicated to building the citadel in Susa, and the king was also a passionate advocate of the Linear Elamite script, encouraging people to use the original Elamite language when the Akkadians tried to force their cultural identity onto the people of Elam.

Although Puzur-Inshushinak strove for cultural and political freedoms and the independence of Elam, it only lasted during his lifetime. After Puzur-Inshushinak's death, the Linear Elamite script was forgotten and fell out of use. Susa fell into the hands of the Neo-Sumerian Empire, also known as the Third Dynasty of Ur. The founder of the Third Dynasty of Ur, Ur-Nammu, who ruled from 2112 BCE to 2095 BCE, was the one to put an end to Elamite sovereignty. Ur-Nammu's son and heir, Shulgi, continued his father's policies. Shulgi even went on to marry the daughters of rulers who controlled the eastern territories of Elam to strengthen his power in the region.

The Shimashki dynasty emerged around 2200 BCE, although it didn't become dominant until 2100 BCE. It began with an unnamed king, whose reign is veiled in mystery, as is the other kings of this dynasty. The Susa king list names fourteen other kings. The dates are obscure, and there is no information found about the reigns of these kings in other sources. Thus, historians suggest these were not sequential rulers and that the dynasty was an alliance of people from different Elamite cultures.

The Shimashki dynasty's rule over Elam, which lasted from around 2100 BCE to 1900 BCE, coincided with the Third Dynasty of Ur. In 2028 BCE, Ur was led by Ibbi-Sin, who would become the last ruler of the Third Dynasty of Ur. The Shimashki military ravaged the kingdom of Ur, looting its riches and destroying its capital. The Shimashki dynasty ruled over the fallen empire for a little over two decades. After the fall of the Third Dynasty of Ur, Shimashki entered more conflicts with Larsa, a city-state around twenty-five kilometers (fifteen and a half miles) southeast of Uruk, and Isin, another Sumerian city, located around thirty-two kilometers (almost twenty miles) south of Nippur. The Shimashki dynasty brought Elam on top, which was what their predecessors had wanted. Under the Shimashki, Elam became one of the richest and most powerful kingdoms in the area of West Asia. Their successors, the Sukkalmah dynasty, continued to rule over the mighty kingdom of Elam. At the time, Syria and Mesopotamia were under the influence of Elam, at least in the commercial, diplomatic, and military sense.

The Sukkalmah dynasty was formed around 1900 BCE, presumably by King Ebarat. Although Shilhaha is the name listed as the founder of the dynasty, historians believe Shilhaha and Ebarat to be the same person. There are thirty rulers recorded on the list of Sukkalmah kings, but little is known about them. Perhaps the most prominent king of the dynasty, aside from the dynasty's founder Ebarat, was King Siwe-Palar-Khuppak, who ruled around 1778 BCE. The king formed diplomatic relations with Hammurabi of Babylon and Zimri-Lim of Mari to conquer Eshnunna, a city-state in central Mesopotamia. His ambition was so great that he wanted to establish his power in Babylon as well, which is when his coalition turned against him. The others drove the Elamites from Eshnunna, putting an end to their influence in Mesopotamia. Little is known about the later kings of the Sukkalmah dynasty, even though the dynasty ended more than a century after Hammurabi turned against Siwe-Palar-Khuppak.

Culture, Government, and Military of Elam

In the earliest times of the Elamites, there was an overlord who would oversee smaller regions of the Elamite territory. Vassal princes governed these smaller regions in the name of the ruling overlord. Despite the general tradition in the lands of the Fertile Crescent, where the firstborn son would inherit the throne, power, and wealth after the king's death, the Elamites had viceroys who would fill that role. The viceroy was usually the overlord's eldest brother. If the overlord died, the viceroy would become the next ruler. If the viceroy died, and there were no brothers left to take over the role, one of the vassal princes would be named as the next overlord. If the overlord's wife became a widow, she wouldn't serve as a queen regent; instead, she would be remarried to the overlord's brother—the future overlord—or marry a vassal prince who would inherit the throne. Their son wouldn't have inheritance rights, as brothers or vassal princes were the ones to take on the power and wealth that came with the throne. In that case, the former vassal prince would be able to name his son or nephew as his successor, leaving the rule over the Elamite territory in the family and starting a new royal dynasty of overlords. This type of governance was complex and complicated when it came to checks, control, and inheritance rights, which was why the Elamites later turned to father-son inheritance, keeping the power close in the family.

The Elamites had a terrestrial army that didn't number more than over a thousand soldiers, although it is possible the Elamites just had a smaller army in the early days. The kingdom might have had its own navy; however, this presumption is not historically confirmed with any accuracy. It is also unknown whether there was a difference between the standing army and the professional one, as well as whether soldiers were fighting voluntarily or were commissioned to defend the kingdom and engage in battles.

According to some archaeologists, Susa was an extension of the Sumerian city-state of Uruk before it became the capital of Elam. Susa can be easily reimagined by visiting the site thousands of years later, as the ancient city, now dead and buried in ancient history, still offers a glimpse into its former glory. Susa still has a magnificent platform rising in the center of the city, complete with ceramic vessels that once offered sacrifices to the gods. The platform used to be a temple, and hundreds of graves rose up around the base of the building. Archaeologists suggest the founding of Susa was conditioned by the destruction of Chogha Mish, which was a nearby settlement, and the abandonment of nearby villages. Judging by the way the ceramics were painted from this period, and as concluded by the artifacts that were excavated thousands of years later, the region was strongly influenced by Mesopotamian culture and during the period before Susa became an integral part of the Uruk period in Mesopotamia. Later on, in the middle of the 4th millennium, Susa became the capital of Elam.

Unlike Mesopotamia in the late 4th millennium and the beginning of the 3rd millennium, ancient Iran didn't become literate all at once. However, lowland Khuzestan, where the people of Elam lived, developed a national identity by creating their very first alphabet. Surprisingly, even though a great part of this region was influenced by Mesopotamian culture and the Uruk period, Elamite emerged as an isolated language that can't be linked to any other language. Since Elam had a fascination with different cultures, it wasn't easy for the Elamites to develop their own language and alphabet and to form a unique identity in the ancient world. As a language isolate, Elamite language cannot be compared to any other known language, which is why its interpretation is often difficult. The Elamite language uses cuneiform, much like Akkadian; however, these languages don't share the same morphology. Out of 20,000 cuneiform clay tablets that represent the opus of the Elamite writing, the majority were economic records.

With the development of literacy and material power, Elam established federal governance. The strength of Elam was seen in its governance, as it held all these lesser states together and efficiently utilized the resources each state had.

Chapter 4 – Anatolia: The Bridge Between Asia and Europe and the Rise of the Hittite Old Kingdom

From prehistoric times, Anatolia, which made up most of modern-day Turkey, was the birthplace to many civilizations. After all, it was a strategic region, as Anatolia represented the bridge between Europe and Asia. The first serious attempt to create a civilized nation in Anatolia is noted to have occurred in the late 4th millennium BCE, which happened alongside the arrival of metallurgy in the Early Bronze Age. The Kura-Araxes, a Transcaucasian culture, brought bronze metallurgy to Anatolia. However, unlike the Fertile Crescent, which had already given birth to kings and soon-to-be emperors, Anatolia remained "trapped" in prehistoric times. This is why we don't hear stories of great wars and spilled blood among the people who lived in this region before the rise of the Akkadian Empire.

Sargon of the Akkadian dynasty is the one responsible for breaking the prehistoric cycle in Anatolia. After Sargon rose to power, he took an interest in Anatolia, as he wanted to use the region to export valuable materials for manufacturing. That is how Anatolia surrendered to a far more powerful region of the Fertile Crescent and became heavily influenced by Akkadian culture. According to the epic Mesopotamian tale of Sargon the Great, known as the *King of Battle*, a campaign was led against the Anatolian city Purushanda, located in central Anatolia, south of the Kızılırmak River. The motive behind the campaign was to protect Akkadian merchants. Although Sargon didn't conquer all of Anatolia, the Akkadian culture stuck around long after Sargon died, lasting until the Guti defeated the last ruler of the Akkadian royal line and took over the empire.

Driven by climate changes, the lack of manpower in the military, hunger, and constant discontent due to the worsening living conditions in the once-great Akkadian Empire, the Guti were able to come in and tear down the great Mesopotamian power. With that move, the influence of the Akkadian Empire in Anatolia slowly but steadily faded away. The Guti were vanquished by another super force: the Assyrian Empire. With the start of Ur-Nammu's reign, who ascended the throne in 2112 BCE as the founder of the Third Dynasty of Ur, the Guti were driven away from the remains of the Akkadian Empire. Anatolia was a part of this claim, and the Assyrians took them over during the Middle Bronze Age. The Assyrians were mostly interested in the silver that could be found in Anatolia. Up until the end of the Middle Bronze Age, Anatolia remained under the influence and rule of the Assyrian Empire.

However, empires rise and fall, and by the end of the Middle Bronze Age, a new kingdom would emerge in Anatolia to take over the region and establish a new cultural identity: the Hittite Old Kingdom. This kingdom would change the political scene in Anatolia by taking over Hattusa, making it the capital of a new Anatolian empire. The entrance of the city was framed with a sphinx gate and was surrounded by rich, lush landscapes, so it is no wonder that the people of Hittite chose Hattusa as the capital of the Hittite Old Kingdom.

However, before the Hittites arrived in Anatolia from the lands beyond the Black Sea, the Hattians lived in central Anatolia. Evidence of Hattians inhabiting this area of Anatolia date all the way back to the influence of the Akkadian Empire and Sargon, around 2350 BCE. The influence of the Hattians was so deeply established in this region that central Anatolia was known as the "Land of the Hatti." Like in the other parts of Anatolia, the Land of the Hatti was defeated and heavily influenced by the Akkadian Empire and, later, the Assyrian Empire. The land of the Hattians was organized into several smaller city-states, in which theocracy ruled. This meant the Hattians believed that their ruler was assigned by the gods or was even related to the gods. The authority of such a ruler was never questioned, as his word was considered to be the word of the gods. The Hattians and Hittites were often confused for being the same people with the same origin, even though that was not the case. This confusion might be due to the assimilation of the Hattians once the Hittites arrived in Anatolia. The Hittites also addressed their kingdom as the "Land of the Hatti," which might have contributed to the misunderstanding. The Hittites arrived in north-central Anatolia around 1600 BCE. About 200 years later, the Hittites would rule over most of Anatolia, the northern Levant, and Upper Mesopotamia.

The Rise of the Hittites in Ancient Anatolia

It is thought that the Hittites arrived from the region of today's Ukraine. To help confirm that theory, the language of the Hittites, which gradually assimilated with that of the Hattians, was a form of an Indo-European language. Although it was far different from the language the Hattians used, the language of the Hittites became a part of the culture of Anatolia.

The story of the Anatolian Hittites starts with King Anitta. King Anitta arrived in north-central Anatolia around 1600 BCE with his people and the Hittite military. The conquest of the region began with the sacking of Hattusa and the Kussara kingdom. The exact borders of Kussara remain unknown, as the city has never been found. Before that moment, Hattusa was the most powerful and richest city of Hatti, and it had stood its ground since 2500 BCE. Hattusa was even successfully defended from Sargon of Akkad and his grandson, Naram-Sin, but it didn't stand a chance against Anitta, who ruled Kussara around the 17th century BCE. King Anitta burned the city down and is said to have cursed it and anyone who ever attempted to rebuild it. The city was rebuilt a generation later by Hattusili I, the founder of the Hittite Old Kingdom, who reigned from 1650 BCE to 1620 BCE. Hattusili means "the one from Hattusa." Archaeologists once argued that the founder of the Hittite line was also known as Labarna I, in which case his son and successor would have been known as Labarna II. However, *labarna* was actually a title rather than a name.

Hattusili didn't stop at rebuilding the city of Hattusa, which happened sometime during his reign. He also decided to extend the domain of his people to the Black Sea and the Mediterranean Sea, expanding the territory of the Hittites in the first year of his reign. In his second year, King Hattusili conquered Alalakh and several other cities in Syria. Hattusili was an ambitious king, and he continued his war campaigns, arriving at Arzawa in western Anatolia in the third year of his reign.

While the king was away on his campaigns, the Hurrians occupied the cities he previously subdued in Syria. The Hurrians lived in Anatolia, Syria, and Mesopotamia, but their most powerful kingdom was known as Mitanni. The Mitanni kingdom was associated with horses, as this animal was highly respected in the Hurrian culture. King Hattusili spent the next three years retaking the cities in Syria that he had previously conquered. There is no further evidence of King Hattusili's reign, although it is known he ruled longer than six years.

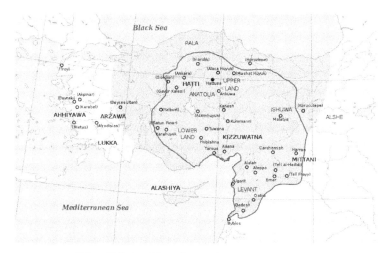

The Hittite Empire at its greatest extent

(https://images.app.goo.gl/zdSqP98JgyEm5eTKA)

Hattusili's reign was harsh, as he had complete control over the lives of his subjects. He was known for punishing deeds he considered to be wrong with the death sentence. At times, his justice was merciless, even when his children were involved.

Before we delve into that, let us look at the family life of Hattusili. Sadly, not much is known about the woman to whom the king was married. It is known that her name was Tawananna. The name of Hattusili's wife would become the title that all Hittite queens would take. Having a queen wasn't just a formality, for the queen held power in case of the king's absence. If the king was away on war campaigns, the queen would then rule the kingdom with full control over the subjects. The queen also had the role of the high priestess, while the king was the high priest. The queen could also perform diplomatic duties, but her official duties were mostly religious. However, the succession of the throne wouldn't go to the queen after the king died. Instead, the first son would become the successor to the throne. In case the first son wasn't able to take the throne, the second son would be named as the successor. In case the king didn't have any sons, he would name his son-in-law as the next ruler, in which case the king's daughter would become Tawananna.

Hattusili had named his nephew, his sister's son, as his successor. The king went off to war with the city of Halab, which was the capital of Yamhad (an ancient Semitic kingdom), destroying it so badly that Halab would never retrieve its glory. All of Hattusili's conquests took place in the first three years of his reign, while he spent the next three in reclaiming the territories from the Hurrians. However, Hattusili returned with severe wounds that could have quickly turned fatal. His nephew seemed to be uncaring about the king's predicament. Despite the king's fierce and sometimes merciless rule, he became furious about how cold his successor was. King Hattusili concluded that it was wrong to have named his nephew, who became his adopted son, as the heir to the throne, as the prince did not shed a tear over Hattusili's possible death. Instead of listening to and caring about Hattusili, the adopted prince, known to history as "Young Labarna," listened to his brothers, sisters, and mother. These people were not teaching the young heir the proper way of kingship, at least in Hattusili's eyes. The king even used to call his sister "the snake." The king couldn't take this disobedience of his adopted son any longer. He exiled him, granted him the title of a priest, and sent him to an estate.

Renouncing Young Labarna wasn't the only time the king was disappointed and betrayed by his own blood. His actual son joined the people of Tappassanda (unknown location) to conspire against the king. Hattusili's son planned the uprising, which included the demise of his own father. The people of Tappassanda joined in on the conspiracy because they would receive an exemption from taxes. The betrayal of his son and later his daughter, who conspired against him so that her son could take the throne, was what made up the king's mind to adopt his nephew and name him the heir to the throne in the first place.

Despite all of this backstabbing, the king finally found an heir he thought would be the perfect successor to the throne: one of his young grandsons, Mursili. Mursili I inherited the throne around 1620 BCE, and since he was a minor, he wouldn't go on war campaigns for three years. Hattusili appears to have chosen the perfect successor, as Mursili, once he came of age, decided to follow in his grandfather's footsteps when it came to conquest. Mursili went on to reclaim the cities in northern Syria, and he also conquered the Yamhad kingdom and its capital, Halab (modern-day Aleppo). From there, he headed out on an ambitious conquest, going forward with his military 2,000 kilometers (a little over 1,240 miles) into the very center of Mesopotamia. The goal was to attack, raid, and sack Babylon. Although the motivation behind the attack is not quite clear to historians, it is thought the king perhaps wanted to take Babylon's grain, as the Hittite crops were destroyed by the Thera eruption (a major volcanic eruption on the island of Thera around 1600 BCE). The king was so successful in his conquest of Babylon that he brought an end to the Amorite dynasty. When Mursili returned to his kingdom after sacking Babylon, he was assassinated, which happened sometime around 1526 BCE. Despite the king's exceptional conquests and war strategies, Hantili, his brother-in-law, and Zidanta, Hantili's son-in-law, sought the king's death. Hantili was also the king's cupbearer, and he was the one who would rule the kingdom after Mursili's death.

During his reign, Hantili I managed to lose the territory in Syria that Mursili had conquered, while the central rule started to lose its power. The rule of Hantili was marked with social decay and uncertainty. His military conquests, or attempted conquests, cost him territories that his predecessors had ruled. Hantili, who ruled for thirty years, was succeeded by Zidanta I, who ruled for ten years. According to the preserved written sources, Zidanta I was not the rightful heir to the throne—at least not while Pisheni, the legitimate heir, and his children existed. Toward the end of Hantili's life, Zidanta killed Pisheni and his children so he could assure the throne for himself.

Almost as if it was a tradition, Zidanta I was also killed, and by the hand of his own son, Ammuna, no less. Zidanta was married to one of Hantili's daughters, which is how the royal line was preserved, for

Ammuna was a child from that marriage. King Ammuna appears to have been even less capable in military strategy and warfare than his father. During his reign, Ammuna lost a substantial amount of territory held by the Hittite Old Kingdom. The king had a daughter, Istapariya, and a son, Huzziya. Ammuna might have had two more sons who were older than Huzziya—Hantili and Tittiya—and they had the right to the throne over Huzziya. However, the relations between Hantili and his supposed sons have never been confirmed with any certainty. Huzziya is said to have organized a series of assassinations to inherit the right to rule. So, once again, the new king came to power through murder and conspiracy.

The next successor and the last king of the Hittite Old Kingdom was Telipinu. Telipinu was married to Istapariya, Ammuna's daughter, which means that Huzziya was his brother-in-law. Telipinu wanted to stop the bloodshed, but he was still motivated by the hunger for power, and he couldn't avoid his fate by following in his predecessors' footsteps. Thus, Huzziya and his supposed brothers were all killed, together with King Telipinu's son and wife. Due to all of the murders that had taken place before his reign, as well as the great loss of territory with each new king that came to the throne, King Telipinu decided to create an edict that would prevent murder for the sake of inheriting the throne. King Telipinu was able to recover some of the lost lands from Mitanni and the Hurrians by allying with the Hurrians of Kizzuwatna. After Telipinu died, the kingdom entered a period that would last for seventy years, known as the Middle Kingdom or the "Dark Ages."

Chapter 5 – The Levant: The Kingdom of Ebla and the Cultures of the Ancient Levant

With Mesopotamia on the east and set between the Mediterranean Sea and the Arabian Desert, the "land of the rising sun" gave birth to some of the first nomadic tribes in the Stone Age. From 8500 BCE to 7000 BCE, numerous settlements were formed in all parts of the Levant, an area that included modern-day Syria, Lebanon, Jordan, Palestine, Israel, and most of Turkey. The domestication of dogs and other animals, as well as plants and grain, has been recorded in these parts. By 6000 BCE, the climate started to change, and settlements began shifting to a nomadic way of life. Groups of hunters and gatherers emerged, and they tended to be influenced by the culture of Egypt, at least judging by the pottery found in the Levant.

The Early Bronze Age corresponds to the Early Syrian Period, a period when several mighty kingdoms ruled the Levant. The First Eblaite Kingdom, the Kingdom of Nagar, and the Second Mariote (Mari) Kingdom dominated the Early Syrian Period, which is around the time when the Akkadians established numerous cities in northern Sumer, around 3500 BCE to 3000 BCE. Ebla was one of the earliest kingdoms in the region of Syria, and it began as a modest settlement in the Levant at the beginning of 3500 BCE. Although it started as a small settlement, Ebla would soon become an unparalleled trading empire. Ebla traded with Sumer, Egypt, Cyprus, and Afghanistan. Instead of borrowing a language from one of these cultures, the people of Ebla had their own language, Eblaite, which is an extinct Semitic language that had been used in the region since the 3rd millennium BCE.

Ebla might have emerged as a part of the Kish civilization that arrived in the western Levant from central Mesopotamia in the mid-4th millennium BCE. The city of Ebla was established around 3500 BCE, and it was built on an outcrop of limestone, which was how Ebla got its name, as it is thought that Ebla means "white rock." Ebla would soon become one of the most powerful kingdoms in the region.

The Rise and Fall of Ebla and Other Ancient Syrian Kingdoms

Although the names of the kings who ruled Ebla during the era of the First Eblaite Kingdom are known to history, there is very little information on some of their reigns. The First Eblaite Kingdom was founded by Sakuma, who started his reign around 3100 BCE, about 400 years after Ebla was founded as a small settlement and over 600 years before the First Eblaite Kingdom would meet its demise. Very little is known about the first king of Ebla. History knows very little about his successors as well, whose names were discovered in the mid-20th century. With the reign of King Sagisu, which commenced around 2680 BCE, more information became available on the royal names and the kings' reigns.

Soon, Ebla became a powerful kingdom with favorable connections with Mesopotamia, southern Syria, and central Anatolia. Not long after this, a hundred-year war with Mari, a Syrian city-state, would begin.

Northwest of the Euphrates riverbank, the people of Mari, under King Ansud, began preparing their attack on the First Eblaite Kingdom. Ansud would later become known as the earliest attested king in the history of the Mari kingdom. Before Mari became a military force to be reckoned with, Mari was a small settlement, much like Ebla. The settlement was abandoned around 2500 BCE for unknown reasons, possibly due to the floods in the area that couldn't be prevented with the major canals that had been previously built in the region. The people of Mari returned a half-century later to repopulate the city, after which Mari became a kingdom that was nearly as powerful as Ebla.

The First Eblaite Kingdom at its greatest extent including vassal states

(https://images.app.goo.gl/WGPDr2SEh97J3bfB8)

Around the end of 2416, under the reign of Sa'umu, Mari would continue the war with Ebla. King Sa'umu launched a series of attacks on many cities of the First Eblaite Kingdom, which gave Mari the upper hand. Kun-Damu, who was the king of Ebla during Sa'umu's reign, managed to defeat Mari.

Kun-Damu's successor, Adub-Damu, is almost unknown to history except for his name, so little is known about his reign. However, more is known about the successor of the Mari kingdom's throne, Ishtup-Ishar, as he continued the path set by his predecessors by conquering two Eblaite cities and continuing the war. While Adub-Damu might have had troubles with defending the kingdom of Ebla, his successor, Igriš-Halam, or Igriš-Halab (*š is pronounced as "sh"*), led a victory against the Mari kingdom, which led to the expansion beyond the city of Halab. It is thought that his other name might be a commemoration of driving the Mari away from Halab.

However, Igriš-Halam's reign is best remembered by his capitulation to Mari. King Iblul-II was on the throne of the Mari kingdom, and he is said to have been one of the most energetic kings that the kingdom ever saw. Iblul-II was interested in conquering the Eblaites, as well as their vassals and allies. King Iblul-II noticed that the Eblaite king was increasing the military and setting out on ambitious campaigns. To stop their expansion, King Iblul-II blocked the trade route that Ebla used with Kish and Nagar. King Iblul-II, also known as "the King of Mari Abarsal," continued his ravaging campaigns across the region, and Ebla was forced to pay a shameful tribute to the Mari kingdom. Iblul-II received a great amount of silver and gold as a result, and he continued to conquer the cities of Ebla, which consequently weakened the Eblaites.

After twelve years of ruling the Eblaite throne, Igriš-Halam was succeeded by his son, Irkab-Damu, who proved to be a far more vigorous king, as he wished to retrieve the old glory of the kingdom of Ebla. Irkab-Damu succeeded the throne around 2340 BCE and ruled for eleven years. During his reign, Ebla became a dominant power in the Levant. King Irkab-Damu started his rule by settling a peace treaty between Abarsal, which was a part of the Mari kingdom, located east of Ebla alongside the riverbank of the Euphrates. The king's goal was to put an end to the tribute given to Mari, so he planned to attack. Nizi, the successor of Iblul-II, was not nearly as skillful in combat and military strategy as his predecessor. This is how Irkab-Damu defeated the Mari kingdom and established Ebla as a powerful force in the region. During the eleven-year reign of Irkab-Damu, Ebla was expanded to its greatest extent, about half the size of modern-day

Syria. Half of the kingdom was controlled directly by the king and his district administrators, while the other half was run by Eblaite vassals. The kingdom of Ebla also developed diplomatic relationships with surrounding city-states and kingdoms, which included Egypt and Hamazi (an ancient city-state whose location is unknown). A letter that was sent to King Zizi of Hamazi testifies that Irkab-Damu sent gifts to the king, asking for mercenaries in return. Irkab-Damu referred to Zizi as his "brother," which further shows the close relationship between the two kings. The gifts from the ruler of Egypt also indicate the political and diplomatic reach of Ebla.

During Irkab-Damu's reign, the vizier would become more important in the political affairs of the kingdom. This would happen mostly in the last two years of his reign, for this was when Vizier Ibrium saw his own rise to power before Irkab-Damu's son, Isar-Damu, took over the throne around 2320 BCE. Isar-Damu's mother, Dusigu, who married the king in the fifth year of his reign, was actually related to Vizier Ibrium. Since Isar-Damu inherited the throne at a very young age, probably when he was six or seven years old, the vizier would become the king's chief official. Irkab-Damu had other sons who were older, so this succession was most likely due to Queen Dusigu's interference, as she was one of her husband's favorite consorts. Her decision wasn't a mistake, for Ebla remained strong under her son's rule, which lasted for thirty-five years.

Isar-Damu continued his father's wars, but he also established a strong diplomatic system, which may have helped Ebla stay on top. While Isar-Damu was still very young, his mother and Vizier Ibrium ruled by his side, during which time the vizier led campaigns against the rebellious vassals of the kingdom. During Isar-Damu's reign, Ebla concluded an alliance with Nagar, which resulted in a marriage between Princess Tagrish-Damu, Isar-Damu's daughter, and the prince of Nagar, Ultum-Huhu. In the hopes of defeating the Mari kingdom once and for all, Isar-Damu allied with Nagar and Kish. At the head of the campaign was the son of Vizier Ibrium, Ibbi-Sipish, who became the new vizier after his father's death. After their victory near Terqa, the king and his allies attacked Armi, a rebellious vassal city of Ebla. King Isar-Damu is considered to be the last king of the First Eblaite Kingdom, although his son, Ir'ak-Damu, who was married to Vizier Ibbi-Sipish's daughter, ascended to the throne for a brief period.

The last days of the First Eblaite Kingdom were recorded to have happened around 2300 BCE when the kingdom was destroyed for the first time. Since the perpetrator(s) and the cause are still unknown, several theories exist as to what happened. Some believe it might have been Mari seeking revenge, as the destruction happened several years after the Battle of Terqa. However, based on the records of Sargon's grandson Naram-Sin, who went campaigning in the region around this time, the city of Ebla was destroyed by the Akkadians. In the inscriptions of Naram-Sin, it is recorded that the army of the Akkadian Empire destroyed the city of "Ibla," which might be a reference to Ebla. Some archaeologists argue that it was a natural catastrophe. It has been suggested that a fire broke out, as the most significant impact was limited to the palace. There were also no signs of looting, which may provide clear indications that the Akkadians weren't responsible for the destruction.

After the destruction of the city, a new period for the kingdom came about. This is known as the Second Eblaite Kingdom, which lasted from 2300 BCE to 2000 BCE. The second kingdom began with the construction of a new royal palace, which was set in the lower area of the city. A new royal line is also said to have emerged, although they were related to the line of kings who ruled the First Eblaite Kingdom. Very little is known about this period since there is no surviving written evidence on the names of these kings. The kingdom was once again burned around 2000 BCE, and it is thought that this destruction was the result of an invasion by the Hurrians, who arrived in the region around 2030 BCE. A former Eblaite vassal city, Ikinkalis, is said to have led the attack that brought the city and the

Second Eblaite Kingdom to its knees. The Third Eblaite Kingdom emerged from the ashes of the burned city, and once again, a new royal palace was built, along with new temples.

The Third Eblaite Kingdom would last from 2000 BCE to 1600 BCE, starting with the rule of Ibbit-Lim. Since Ibbit-Lim is an Amorite name, it is suggested that the people of Ebla were now Amorites, as were the majority of inhabitants in Syria at the time. The Amorites were a Semitic-speaking people, who would go on to establish a powerful dynasty of Babylon. The list of kings who ruled the Third Eblaite Kingdom appears to be exclusively Amorite. However, the list seems to have severe gaps. Only four names appear on the list, despite the fact the kingdom was around for 400 years. This lack of written evidence takes us to 1750 BCE when the kingdom was ruled by King Immeya, whose full name is not known. What is known is that the king had diplomatic relations with Egypt and Pharaoh Hotepibre of the Thirteenth Dynasty. At the time of Immeya's rule, Ebla had become the vassal of Yamhad, an Amorite kingdom. After the reign of King Immeya, an unknown king came to the throne. Archaeologists have found a partial name for this ruler from a tablet found in the ruins of this city, but nothing else is known about his reign. It has been suggested that his name was Hammurabi, as the partial name is "Hammu." Indillima emerged as the last king of Ebla, and he ruled around 1600 BCE. His son, Maratewari, never had a chance to rule, as the kingdom was destroyed by King Mursili I of the Hittites. The Eblaite kingdom was destroyed, and it never retrieved its previous glory.

Culture, Military, and Government of Ebla

Although it was located near the regions heavily influenced by Sumer and Mesopotamia, the Eblaites managed to preserve their cultural identity through their unique political organization, language, and religion. The deities that were worshiped in this region were specifically related to the Eblaite culture, and women enjoyed great respect, which made the queen an important figure in political and religious affairs.

The city of Ebla had fifty-six hectares of land that were divided into four districts, with each district having its own separate gates and fortifications. The city had a lower town and an acropolis in the center, where the king's palace was built. The city also had two temples, and the kings were buried outside the city in royal tombs. The kingdom would go through many transformations and changes in terms of buildings and overall architecture with the Second and Third Eblaite Kingdoms. The government of Ebla had the king as the head of the city-state, but the king didn't rule by himself, as he had a council of elders, administrative divisions, and the grand vizier that all helped make decisions as well. Thirteen court dignitaries oversaw the administrative divisions, and each one controlled between 400 and 800 men. Since the city was divided into four districts, each district had several deputies and one chief inspector, who would oversee the district and report to the king. The king would extend his power to protect royal interests by employing agents, messengers, and collectors. The next in line for the throne, the crown prince, would be included in internal affairs, while the second eldest son was involved in foreign affairs. The queen also had an important role in the kingdom, and her title allowed her to have a vote in the kingdom's matters and internal affairs. The vassal states were autonomous, but they still had to pay tribute to the kingdom and send military assistance upon the king's request.

The settlement of Ebla started to get rich based on trade, especially due to the rising demand for wool in Sumer. The records found in the ancient kingdom testify that the king had many sheep, meaning he had abundant wool to trade. The Eblaites also produced excess food with which to trade. However, the kingdom's economy and financial prosperity were mostly in the hands of villages, which paid their share in taxes to the kingdom. The king would distribute food for all seasonal and permanent workers in the palace. The kingdom mostly lived off pastoral agriculture, while large herds of cattle were kept by the palace and controlled by the king as well.

The language of the Eblaites is known as Eblaite or Paleo Syrian, and this language belongs to the group of extinct Semitic languages. Eblaite wasn't only used within the borders of the kingdom, as a modified version of the language was also used in the kingdoms of Mari and Nagar. The majority of Eblaite writing is related to the economy and administration; however, texts with myths and proverbs were also found, as well as bilingual texts written in Eblaite and Sumerian.

Chapter 6 - The Rise of the Assyrian Empire and Babylon from the Ashes of Akkad

The Akkadian Empire fell around 2154 BCE with the arrival of the Guti, who displaced the power of Akkad in the Fertile Crescent by taking advantage of the civil wars and droughts that had created an explosive and tense atmosphere in the empire. Descending from the Zagros Mountains as a tribal conglomerate, the Guti sought the prosperity that could be found in the plains of Mesopotamia, Sumer, and the surrounding regions. The Guti conquered Akkad by demoralizing their troops, as they looted and destroyed everything with a "hide-and-seek" strategy, in which the Guti would attack a city then move onto the next one before the military could even arrive. Working in the fields and traveling became unsafe due to the Guti. All of this resulted in fear and famine in the cities of the former Akkadian Empire.

At the time, the Guti were ruled by a nameless king, and while they moved across the region, conquering and looting, some of the city-states that belonged to the Akkadian Empire managed to survive and remain untouched by the tribe from the Zagros Mountains. Lagash was one such place, as it continued to thrive under the ruling hand of a local dynasty.

It is perhaps unimaginable for a modern-day reader to understand the horror of the Mesopotamians, who were facing famine, droughts, and internal conflicts when the Guti arrived. The Guti were described as subnormal beings without religion and an unwillingness to conform to the laws and customs of the civilized world. They are described by the Mesopotamians as animals who spoke a language that sounded much like babbling. The Guti released the domestic animals kept by the people so they could roam freely, and they knew nothing about irrigation and agriculture. This contributed to the dark ages of Mesopotamia, where everyone ruled but no one was king. The Guti weren't able to lead in a civilized world, as they knew nothing about politics or even complex canal networks. As a result, their rule was crude and disorganized. Their inability to rule a civilized world with complex organization swept prosperity away from the region, which resulted in a great number of deaths caused by famine.

After the death of Shar-Kali-Sharri of Akkad, the Sumerian King List names four different kings in only three years, indicating an intense turnover of power in the kingdom. After them, the list goes on to name nine more kings, who ruled for a combined sixty-five years. The Gutian hordes were led by nameless kings, with a total of twenty-one Gutian kings for ninety-one years. One of the Gutian kings ruled for only forty days, which perfectly describes the political climate of the Mesopotamian dark ages.

The Assyrians were subjects of the Akkadian Empire before its fall, and they managed to gain independence with the arrival of the Gutian hordes. It didn't last, for after the founding of the Neo-Sumerian Empire, otherwise known as the Third Dynasty of Ur, which happened around 2112 BCE, the Assyrian city of Ashur fell under the influence of the new Sumerian power. However, Nineveh and the far north remained untouched.

The Third Dynasty of Ur

During the Sumerian renaissance, the Guti were driven out of the region by the king of Uruk, Utu-Hengal. His son-in-law, Ur-Nammu, would become the founder of the Third Dynasty of Uruk. Utu-Hengal came to power over Uruk in 2120 BCE and ruled until 2112 BCE. Utu-Hengal defeated the last Gutian king, Tirigan, which signaled the end of the Gutian era and the Mesopotamian dark ages. Utu-Hengal is considered to be the direct predecessor to the Third Dynasty of Uruk, and he was looked upon as a great hero by the Sumerian people. Utu-Hengal even carried the title characteristic for the kings of Akkad, "the king of the four quarters," also known as the "king of the world." The king's daughter married his successor, Ur-Nammu, so the crown of Ur stayed in the royal family.

Ur-Nammu came to the throne in 2112 BCE. During this time, the Assyrians were largely under the influence of Sumer and the Third Dynasty of Ur. Although the dynasty was officially founded by Ur-Nammu, his father-in-law had set a solid ground for the development of a strong dynasty. The Guti and their reign of chaos were gone, and the cities of Sumer, including Uruk, could now reestablish their power and glory. Around half a century after the foundation of the Neo-Sumerian Empire, the Assyrians would become vassal governors of the Ur dynasty.

Ur-Nammu continued on to conquer Susa and built the wall of Ur in the third year of his reign. He would then receive the kingship from Nippur, where he would later build the temple of Nanna. The Guti weren't truly defeated until the seventh year of his reign. After completely destroying the Guti, Ur-Nammu dedicated his rule to restoring the general order in the region, focusing on trade, roads, rebuilding temples and the looted, decaying cities, and reconquering territories in central and northern Mesopotamia. Ur-Nammu also created the oldest preserved code of law, known as the Code of Ur-

Nammu. This code, which was written in Sumerian, regulated the lives of the people, including slaves and free people.

Ur-Nammu ruled until 2095 BCE, after which he was succeeded by his son, Shulgi. Shulgi is said to have ruled for forty-eight years, finishing most of what his father had started during his reign and strengthening the dominance of the dynasty in the region and beyond. He even received the title of divinity in the thirty-third year of his reign. Shulgi continued with his father's work of modernizing the kingdom, which led to writing reforms, reorganizations of the army, major reconstruction projects, and tax reforms. After a long and fruitful reign, Shulgi was succeeded by Amar-Sin in 2047 BCE.

During the rule of Amar-Sin, Ushpia would become the first independent king of Assyria, although some records mention a King Zariqum, who is claimed to have been the governor of Ashur during the reign of Amar-Sin. Amar-Sin extended the borders of the Neo-Sumerian Empire to the northern provinces of Hamazi and Lullubi, and these provinces were assigned governors to protect royal interests. His reign ended in 2038 BCE. He was succeeded by his brother, Shu-Sin. Shu-Sin reigned until 2029 BCE, which was only several years before the rise of the Old Assyrian Empire in 2025 BCE. During the first year of his reign, Shu-Sin had to deal with the rebellion of his Amorite subjects, and he decided to build a fortified wall between the Tigris and Euphrates to prevent more potential Amorite offenses. He was succeeded by his son, Ibbi-Sin, who would reign from 2027 BCE to 2002 BCE.

Ibbi-Sin was the last ruler of the Neo-Sumerian Empire, as the Third Dynasty of Ur was about to fall. Over the years, the Assyrians had slowly been recollecting to form an independent kingdom. Ibbi-Sin decided to campaign against Elam, which was how he met his demise. The king didn't make it far into the Elamite lands. The Elamites defeated the king, took him captive, and ultimately destroyed the Neo-Sumerian Empire and the Third Dynasty of Ur. It was time for the Amorites, who had slowly gained power over the years, to rise up and establish their influence in Mesopotamia. Although they first introduced a semi-nomadic lifestyle to the people, the Amorites soon built a merchant empire, establishing independent dynasties in the city-states of southern Mesopotamia, among which were Lagash, Eshnunna, Larsa, Isin, and later Babylon.

After the demise of the Third Dynasty of Ur, Puzur-Ashur I, whose name is translated as "the servant of Ashur," began his reign over Assyria, ruling until 1950 BCE. He was succeeded by his son, Shalim-Ahum, meaning "keeping the brothers safe." This name might show the determination of the Assyrians to gain back their independence and reestablish their cultural identity while defying potential attacks from neighboring city-states. He reigned until 1900 BCE and was succeeded by Illu-Shuma, his son, after which Erishum I, the son of Illu-Shuma, came to the throne. He began his rule in 1905 BCE and ruled until 1876 BCE. Erishum I expanded the borders of the Assyrian Empire while building new temples, walls, and fortifications. The king also established *karums*—"trading posts"— along the trading routes of Anatolia. Erishum also revised the code of law and established tax exemptions for the remission of debts, which could be paid in silver, gold, or even wool. He even allowed plaintiffs to be represented by attorneys.

Erishum was succeeded by his brother, Ikunum, who reigned from 1867 BCE to 1860 BCE, which was more than a half a century before the Old Assyrian Empire would meet the rising power of Babylon. The king further fortified the city of Ashur and continued to maintain the trading colonies along the Anatolian trade route. Ikunum was succeeded by his son, who carried the name of the first emperor in history. Sargon I, "the steward of Ashur," ruled for thirty-nine years until 1821 BCE. His son, Puzur-Ashur II, came to the throne at an old age, as his father ruled for almost forty years. Puzur-Ashur named his son Naram-sin, after the grandson of Sargon of Akkad, which might show the desire for the Assyrians to identify with the once-glorious Akkadian Empire. The dynasty of Puzur-Ashur I ended with

Naram-sin's successor, Erishum II. Erishum II would rule the kingdom from 1815 BCE to 1809 BCE. He was deposed by the usurper Shamshi-Adad I.

Shamshi-Adad I of the Amorites conquered the Old Assyrian Empire, Upper Mesopotamia, most of Syria, and the Levant. Shamshi-Adad ascended as the first Amorite king of Assyria, although he claimed to be related to Ushpia to legitimize his right to the Assyrian throne. His son and successor, Ishme-Dagan I, who came to the throne in 1776 BCE, wasn't a brilliant warlord like his father. Instead, he lost many of the territories his father had conquered during his reign, which included the Levant and southern Mesopotamia. These fell under the influence of the Sumerian city-state of Eshnunna and the Mari kingdom. Ishme-Dagan I was a contemporary to King Hammurabi, who managed to reinforce Babylon as an important power in the region, and the two had tolerable relations. Since Ishme-Dagan's line would continue for three more generations, his successors would witness the rising power of Babylon, which started with the First Amorite Dynasty and King Sumu-abum.

The Rise of Babylon and the First Amorite Dynasty

Before Sumu-abum, Babylon was just a city in Babylonia, which was a kingdom in Mesopotamia. Although Sumu-abum showed no interest in declaring himself as a king of Babylon, he is still known as the first king of the First Babylon (Amorite) Dynasty. He freed Babylon and a small area that belonged to the Amorite city of Kazallu. He also claimed a small administrative center in southern Mesopotamia. Sumu-abum was a chieftain of Babylon from 1894 BCE to 1881 BCE and was succeeded by Sumu-la-El, his son, who would reign from 1881 BCE to 1845 BCE. Four generations later, Hammurabi, the sixth king of the First Dynasty, would establish an empire based in the city of Babylon that would live as long as the king who founded it.

Hammurabi inherited the throne from his father, Sin-Muballit, who had to renounce his position due to falling ill. Hammurabi's reign started around 1792 BCE when he was about eighteen years old, and it lasted for forty-two years, during which he transformed Babylon into a powerful kingdom.

Before Hammurabi came to the throne, Babylon was a rather small city, which, although growing more powerful by the year, was surrounded by mightier neighbors, such as Isin, Eshnunna, Larsa, and Assyria. However, Sin-Muballit conquered a small area in south-central Mesopotamia, which included Kish, Sippar, and Borsippa. When Hammurabi ascended the throne, he was the king of a small kingdom with a fairly complex geopolitical situation. Regardless of the more powerful kingdoms and their plans for expansion, Babylon didn't enter conflicts with other cities and kingdoms in the first years of Hammurabi's reign. Hammurabi took care of Babylon instead, starting a great number of public works, which included the expansion of temples and improving the city's walls for defensive purposes.

Several years into his reign, around 1783 BCE, the mighty kingdom of Elam decided to invade the Mesopotamian plains with some allies, which led to the conquest of Eshnunna and several smaller cities in the plains. That was the first time Elam invaded this region, and it met with success, partially thanks to its allies. The next target for Elam was Hammurabi's little kingdom and Larsa. Elam didn't attack the two kingdoms directly but instead tried to start a war between the two kingdoms to consolidate power. Instead of battling against one another, the king of Larsa and Hammurabi entered into an alliance to crush the Elamites. Larsa might have been an ally, but the kingdom didn't put any effort into contributing to military power. Despite this, Babylon crushed the Elamites. Hammurabi couldn't forgive the king of Larsa for failing to send military assistance against Elam. So, the king of Babylon decided to attack Larsa and expand into the southern parts of the Mesopotamian plains. He was in control of this region by 1763 BCE.

Hammurabi continued his conquests, as his ambitions didn't stop at defending Babylon from the Elamites and conquering Larsa. Hammurabi took his army to the north, conquering Eshnunna and the kingdom of Mari, even though Mari was one of his allies in a previous campaign. Mari probably surrendered without a battle. After this, Hammurabi entered an extended war with Assyria, which was led by King Ishme-Dagan I. Seeking for a way to gain the upper hand in this war, both sides recruited allies, which included several smaller city-states in the region. Right before the death of Ishme-Dagan I, Hammurabi had finally won the war, and the new king, Mut-Ashkur, the son of Ishme-Dagan, had to pay tribute to Babylon. In only several years, all of Mesopotamia, with the exclusion of Qatna and Aleppo, was under the rule of the mighty Hammurabi. Moreover, Assyria continued to pay tribute to Babylon. Hammurabi even claimed the title "King of the Amorites" after his conquests.

Hammurabi also famously wrote a new code of law, which was fairly different from earlier Sumerian laws. This code of law focused on punishing the perpetrator instead of compensating the victim of the crime. Many of the punishments in the Code of Hammurabi resulted in death. The preface of the code states that Hammurabi was chosen by Shamash, the god of justice that was worshiped in Babylon. During the reign of Hammurabi, Babylon gained the status of being the holiest city in all of Mesopotamia.

However, despite all the might that Babylon had established in the region, the empire lived as long as its driving force. Babylon's short-lived power started to decline with the death of Hammurabi and the rule of his son and successor, Samsu-Iluna, who ascended the throne in 1750 BCE after his father died.

A few years after the death of Hammurabi, the conquered cities under Babylon's control started to rebel. Elam and Assyria were the first among many to start an uprising against the once-mighty kingdom that Hammurabi had founded. However, Hammurabi's son couldn't preserve it. There were many revolts, of which some were successfully extinguished by Samsu-Iluna. However, the chaos that emerged with the numerous rebellions was too much for Hammurabi's successor, leaving the king of Babylon with a fraction of the territory that his father had left him with.

Culture, Government, and Military of the Assyrian Empire

The Assyrian government was a monarchy, and the king was considered to be divinely appointed. The king would rule autonomously, although he wasn't alone in running the affairs of the kingdom. The king had court officials, chief ministers, and servants, who all helped take care of the court. The royal officials mostly belonged to the Assyrian aristocracy. However, some officials had different origins; some were slaves who were granted their freedom, and others had humble backgrounds. Servants were practically the arteries of the court, as they were in charge of everyday chores in the royal palace and ensured everything ran smoothly. Palace officials would control and oversee the servants to make sure everything was in proper order and matching protocols. One of the highest-ranking officials was the royal cupbearer. The cupbearer would share insight into the matters of the kingdom with the king and would certainly have his confidence. Important chief ministers included the chief of the army and the chancellor. There was also a large administrative staff that participated in internal and foreign affairs. The title of the king was hereditary, so the crown prince was proclaimed during the king's life and would be trained to become a king as to be ready when his turn came. The crown prince would learn about war, diplomacy, and politics, including both internal and foreign affairs.

The Assyrian army was based on the early standards of Mesopotamian warfare, referring to the concept of the imperialistic army that Sargon created in the Akkadian Empire. The strength of the Assyrian Empire was solely based on its army's power. Even though Assyrians looked up to the model of Akkadian military forces, the

Assyrians made some warfare innovations. The Assyrian army was the first army in the world to take advantage of weapons and armor made of iron. During the Bronze Age and Early Iron Age, aristocratic soldiers were usually armed better and had chariots for more efficient warfare. However, when iron was used later on in the Iron Age, the Assyrians could efficiently arm common soldiers, as the production of iron armor, weapons, and chariots were cheap since they had accessibility to iron ore. As a result, there were more soldiers in the cavalry and infantry units. The Assyrian army also started to equip its soldiers with more horses, which made chariots moderately redundant, as horse riders were more efficient in combat. Each commander had a permanent army garrison stationed across strategic points in the empire, usually close to the vassal kingdoms to keep the vassals in check. Soldiers voluntarily served the army, and they would be trained in camps before being sent off to campaigns. Common soldiers could be awarded higher ranks based on their service, training, and war contributions.

The Assyrians used the Akkadian language in everyday life, so the early Assyrian language represents a dialect of Akkadian. Sumerian was also used during the Old Assyrian Empire, which lasted between 2025 BCE and 1378 BCE. However, Sumerian was only used by priests for liturgic and religious purposes. The language of trade was Aramaic, which was later adopted by the Assyrians in the Neo-Assyrian Empire around 911 BCE.

Culture, Government, and Military in Hammurabi's Babylon

Hammurabi brought some of the greatest reforms to Babylon. Not only was Hammurabi an exceptional military leader and war strategist, but he was also interested in reforming the law to respond to his vision of justice. This is why he created the Code of Hammurabi. The code didn't only cover the main laws of the kingdom but also addressed everyday life concerns. For instance, the code prescribed fees that needed to be paid for various professional services, such as medical services, for example. The Code of Hammurabi also regulated divorce, marriage, trading, damaged property, inheritance, building standards, and the responsibility of builders for their work. Hammurabi presented the law as given by the god of justice, Shamash, and he took on the role of a righteous king who was gladly getting involved with the legal disputes of his subjects. The Code of Hammurabi was also the first law to include the presumption of innocence, which means that the accused would be treated as innocent until proven guilty. Moreover, there was a social stratification in the laws of the empire based on which punishments, rewards, and legal provisions were made. The social stratification differentiated slaves, free men, and women.

Hammurabi also relied on administration and court officials to practice and execute the laws he had presented as the will of the god of justice. Scribes and scholars were the very basis of his administration, as they recorded everything that was going on within the empire. Running an empire was made more efficient by this and by the number of officials participating in the empire's internal matters. Hammurabi's sons also participated in the empire's affairs, specifically participating in diplomatic missions. Whenever Hammurabi would conquer a new territory, he would send a delegation of officials with one of his sons at the head to peacefully integrate the region.

Hammurabi learned from the past when it came to the way he organized and conducted his warfare tactics. He copied tactics first used by Sargon and used the same weapons and military units as well, taking advantage of composite bows. One of Hammurabi's tactics was to create alliances and then later conquer and subdue them.

Chapter 7 – The Old and New Kingdom of Egypt: Dynastic Egypt and the Rise of Power in the Banks of Nile

With the end of the Predynastic period and the First Dynasty of Egypt, a new dynastic power was about to emerge. With the rise of Hotepsekhemwy, the Second Dynasty was established, in which Upper and Lower Egypt were still unified. Although little is known about this dynasty, records indicate that this was a period of important economic and institutional development that later defined Egypt as a kingdom. Hotepsekhemwy started his reign in 2890 BCE and ruled for around twenty-five years from Thinis, the capital of the kingdom. There is little known about the first pharaoh of the Second Dynasty, but it has been suggested that the pharaoh came to the throne during political turmoil, as indicated by the word "Hotep" in his Horus name, which means "peaceful" or "reconciling."

According to written evidence and royal tablets, Nebra was the next in line. He ruled between ten and fourteen years; however, similar to his predecessor, little is known about his reign. His royal name is given to honor Horus, and it means "Lord of the sun," which signifies the beginning of sun-worshiping in the Egyptian religion. Following the rule of Nebra, the Egyptian throne belonged to Nynetjer, then Senedj, and then Khasekhemwy, who is undisputedly the most well-known pharaoh of the Second Dynasty, as well as the last pharaoh of the dynasty. Khasekhemwy ruled around 2690 BCE for eighteen years. What is important to know about this period is the presence of radical civil wars between Upper and Lower Egypt and the disbalance between the worshipers of the Egyptian deities Horus and Seth, which caused the two regions to split once more. Khasekhemwy stopped these civil wars and reunited Upper and Lower Egypt. After this, Khasekhemwy focused on masonry during his reign. He had several war campaigns during his reign but is most known for the reunification of Egypt and building forts at Abydos and Nekhen.

After the death of Khasekhemwy, the kingdom of Egypt entered a new era once again. This was the Third Dynasty, which introduced the Old Kingdom of Egypt in 2686 BCE. The Old Kingdom was ruled by the Third, Fourth, Fifth, and Sixth Dynasties, ending around 2613 BCE.

Although the records about the end of the Second Dynasty are obscure, it is suggested that Egypt might have gone through a turbulent period, for it was possibly ravaged by civil wars. Djoser was the first pharaoh of the Third Dynasty, and during his reign, the capital was relocated from Thinis to Memphis. Djoser was the son of Khasekhemwy and was also his successor to the throne, although it remains a mystery as to whether he was actually the first in the line. Djoser ended the civil war after ascending to the throne and reuniting Upper and Lower Egypt. The first pharaoh of the Third Dynasty also led a substantial number of expeditions, most notably in the Sinai Peninsula. It is said that he ended the famine in Egypt that had lasted for seven years after rebuilding the temple of Khnum, but his most famous construction project was his step pyramid in Saqqara, where he was buried after his death. He was succeeded by Sekhemkhet in around 2648 BCE, who might have ruled for six or seven years. Very little is known about his reign. The list of the Third Dynasty pharaohs is likewise obscure, as archaeologists are unable to differentiate all the names found on the tablets. Later came Khaba, his son Huni, and then his grandson Sneferu. Sneferu would be the founding pharaoh of the Fourth Dynasty.

Sneferu founded the Fourth Dynasty around 2613 BCE under the Horus name, "Horus has perfected me." He ruled Egypt for at least twenty-seven years, although some archaeologists suggest that he might have ruled longer. He had eight sons and five daughters. Some of his daughters were married to their brothers, probably under a belief of preserving the purity of the royal bloodline. Khufu, Sneferu's successor, who was probably his oldest son, was married to two of his sisters. Khufu's brother's, Ankhhaf and Nefermaat I, served their father as viziers, and Ankhhaf was married to one of his five sisters. During his reign, Sneferu erected the Dahshur pyramids, creating a new standard for building these wondrous monuments that served as royal tombs. By this point, Egypt already had a strong cult of the afterlife, which means that pharaohs, who were believed to be some sort of deity, invested a lot of their wealth, power, and time into planning out their burial places. During the reign of Sneferu, the land became richer, which was how the three pyramids were able to be built, as they demanded substantial human labor. Sneferu made that possible by conquering Nubia and Libya, from where he took a great number of people as slaves and raw materials.

Khufu, also known as Cheops, succeeded his father around 2589 BCE, and he was the commissioner of the Great Pyramid of Giza, which has been preserved for thousands of years and is categorized as one of the Seven Wonders of the Ancient World. The name of the new pharaoh also might point out a bold change in the deity dominance, as he was dedicated to worshiping the god of creation and growth, Khnum. Some archaeologists and Egyptologists point out that

Khufu was Sneferu's son-in-law and that he ascended to the throne by marrying two of Sneferu's daughters.

Khufu was blessed with nine sons and five daughters. His firstborn son, Kawab, was supposed to inherit the throne; however, he died before the pharaoh, so Khufu's successor became his second eldest son: Djedefre. In 2566 BCE, Djedefre ascended the throne. He became the first pharaoh to associate his power and the sacred right to rule with the religious cult of Ra. He introduced the title "Son of Ra," and he later married his older brother's widow. Djedefre was succeeded by his younger brother after he died. Khafra, the new pharaoh, married his brother's widow, the same wife as Kawab. Djedefre continued the tradition by building another pyramid, which would become his resting place. Khafra also built the second-largest pyramid in Giza during his reign, along with one of the most famous ancient Egyptian monuments—the Great Sphinx of Giza. However, it is not known why Djedefre was succeeded by his brother instead of one of his many sons. Khafra was described as a heretic and a cruel ruler by Herodotus 2,000 years later. The same tyrannical reputation followed his father, Khufu, as well.

The successor of Khafra, his son Menkaure, was said to be completely different. Herodotus writes that Menkaure relieved the suffering and pain that his father imposed on his subjects. His father had supposedly enslaved his own people and made them labor for his own prosperity and advantage. Menkaure ruled for around twenty years, starting his reign around 2520 BCE. He didn't have many children compared to his predecessors, as he only had three sons and two daughters. He was succeeded by his younger son, Shepseskaf, the sixth and last pharaoh of the Fourth Dynasty.

While some archaeologists suggest that there was another pharaoh after Shepseskaf, which would have made Shepseskaf the penultimate pharaoh of the dynasty, there is not enough evidence to prove that the presumed pharaoh, Thamphthis, was a pharaoh of the Fourth Dynasty. Thamphthis is recorded as being the next to take the throne, but his name does not appear in any tomb or royal monument, making it unclear who he even was. Thus, it remains uncertain whether the next pharaoh was Thamphthis or Shepseskaf's son Userkaf, who was the founder of the Fifth Dynasty. Userkaf might have been the priest of Ra, as the cult of Ra became stronger and more present during his rule. This elevation of Ra might be another indication that Userkaf wasn't related to the last king of the Fourth Dynasty. For more proof that could help testify this theory, Egyptologists and archaeologists turn to the Westcar Papyrus. The Westcar Papyrus is an ancient Egyptian text that contains stories of magic and wonders. Among these stories, there is a legend about the transition between the Fourth and Fifth Dynasties. This story takes us back to the time when Khufu ruled the kingdom. Khufu was given a prophecy that claimed that he and his heirs would be overthrown by triplets who would be born to the wife of the priest of Ra from Sakhbu.

In the early 25th century BCE, Userkaf was succeeded by Sahure, his son and heir. Sahure's reign would mark the Fifth Dynasty's political and cultural peak. During his reign, Egypt established trading connections with the coastal cities in the Levant. These naval expeditions brought slaves, cedar trees, and numerous exotic items back to Egypt. Egypt was flourishing and changing with the developing trading relations, and the Egyptian navy flourished and developed as well, which included the creation of small racing boats and fleets designed for the high seas. After Sahure's expeditions brought back myrrh, electrum, and malachite from Punt, he led a war campaign against the chieftains of Libya in the Western Desert, which is how livestock was brought back to Egypt. It appeared that the golden age for Egypt had arrived with Sahure and the Fifth Dynasty. His son and successor, Neferirkare Kakai, who ascended the throne in the mid-25th century BCE, is also said to have been a benevolent ruler, and he was succeeded by Shepseskare after ruling for twenty years, but this was only for several months. Shepseskare is believed to have been a younger brother of Neferirkare, and it is unknown if he died of an untimely death or was dethroned for some reason by his nephew, Neferefre, who became the pharaoh after Shepseskare's death. Neferefre died suddenly in his early twenties after only several years on the throne, after which he was succeeded by his younger brother, Nyuserre Ini, who came to power around the late 25th century BCE. He either ruled for twenty-five or thirty-five years. Nyuserre Ini continued with the mining expeditions, and exotic items continued to arrive in Egypt, but very little is known about the military campaigns that might have been led by this pharaoh. However, he remains the most prolific builder of the Fifth Dynasty, as he had six pyramids built during his reign. The pharaoh was succeeded by Menkauhor, his son, whose own son, Djedkare Isesi, took the throne after Menkauhor's death.

Djedkare ruled for at least three decades, and there is some strong evidence that the pharaoh ruled Egypt for forty-four years. To testify his long reign, religious, governmental, and political reforms that placed power in decentralized and provincial administrations can be traced for over four decades. He was the eighth ruler of the Fifth Dynasty, and during his reign, Egypt continued to trade across the Levantine coast. The pharaoh also started expeditions to Sinai, which would bring turquoise and copper to Egypt, and he also took incense from Punt and gold and diorite from Nubia. Djedkare became a part of a religious cult in Egypt that possibly lasted until the very end of the Fifth Dynasty. Djedkare made radical changes to the way the kingdom was governed by decentralizing the ruling control and appointing officials of the kingdom as a part of the new state administration. These reforms placed more power in the hands of officials, but some historians argue these changes brought the Old Kingdom into the dark ages.

Unas, his son, ascended to the throne after his father died in his fifties sometime in the mid-24th century BCE. Unas's reign was marked by economic collapse. The new decentralized administration of the kingdom also continued under his rule, which seemed to add fuel to the pyre of the Fifth Dynasty. Some Egyptologists believe this type of administration allowed the officials to become more powerful, which would contribute to the overall collapse of the Old Kingdom of Egypt almost 200 years later with the last ruler of the Sixth Dynasty. Despite the hardships in the economy, Egypt continued to maintain its trading relations. Unas's death marked the end of an era in Egypt, as the next ruler, Teti, would start the Sixth Dynasty. Evidence found by archaeologists indicates that ancient Egyptians didn't make a distinction between the Fifth and Sixth Dynasties, although we do today for easier accessibility.

Teti might have been married to Unas's daughter, which would have made her one of his three queens. Marrying a royal would explain how Teti came to ascend the throne. He founded what is arguably known as the last dynasty of the Old Kingdom, although some archaeologists consider the Seventh and Eighth Dynasties to be a part of the Old Kingdom era as well. This is because the administration of the later Fifth Dynasty continued in these later dynasties.

Teti had three sons, but he was succeeded by a man named Userkare, who is believed to have murdered the pharaoh to get to the throne. Userkare very well might have been a usurper to the throne since his body wasn't buried in any of the royal tombs. Another theory indicates that Userkare might have ruled until Teti's son came of age, as he succeeded the throne after Userkare. This would have made Userkare an official of the kingdom rather than a usurper.

Pepi I Meryre, Teti's son, inherited the throne in 2331 BCE and ruled for fifty years. At the end of his life, he established a coregency with his son and heir, Merenre I. The consolidation of dynastic power continued with his reign, as Merenre appointed a court official, Weni, as the governor of Upper Egypt. It seems he inherited his predecessor's fascination with Nubia, which is why he continued exploring this land. After his death, Pepi II Neferkare gained control of Egypt, with the power of the governors continuing. Pepi II maintained foreign relations, as he is mentioned in inscriptions written by the Phoenicians. However, his power and the power of the pharaoh as the ruling figure was slowly decaying due to the decentralized governance and administration of the kingdom, as it allowed for the rise of the nobility. These nobles soon started to attack one another due to their ambition to take more territory and become wealthier. Pepi II's son, Merenre II Nemtyemsaf, inherited the throne at a very old age, and he only ruled for a year. By that point, the kingdom was divided into forty-two provinces, and each of these provinces was controlled by a governor who had been appointed by the king.

The power of the pharaohs, which had been established hundreds of years before, was crumbling with the rising ambition and thirst of the Egyptian governors. Herodotus wrote about an Egyptian legend that mentions Queen Nitocris as the last ruler of the Sixth Dynasty. According to the story, she was the wife and sister of Merenre II, who is said to have been killed in a riot. The queen wanted to take revenge, so she drowned all of his murderers during a banquet.

However, there are no records that this queen ever existed, instead attesting Pharaoh Netjerkare Siptah as the last ruler of the dynasty. He is considered to have ruled for only three years before he was succeeded by Menkare. This was when the Old Kingdom came to a violent and dark end, introducing Egypt to the First Intermediate Period, also referred to as the dark ages. Political chaos, looting, the destruction of monuments and temples, and civil wars marked this era. The Egyptian kingdom was now divided into two main powers: Heracleopolis in Lower Egypt and Thebes in Upper Egypt. The kingdom saw the reunification of these two parts once Mentuhotep II ascended to the throne with the Eleventh Dynasty of Egypt, which marked the beginning of the Middle Kingdom.

Mentuhotep II ascended the throne in Thebes, Upper Egypt, while the Tenth Dynasty ruled Lower Egypt as a rivaling power. The Middle Kingdom is also known as the Period of Reunification, as

Mentuhotep II sent his armies to destroy the Tenth Dynasty and conquer Lower Egypt. The conquest took place during the fourteenth year of his reign, and the main trigger for such an action was Lower Egypt's desecration of the ancient necropolis of Abydos, which not only was located in Upper Egypt but was also sacred. Mentuhotep II seemed to have realized the damage that the some-200-year-old administrative reform had brought to the kingdom, for after he defeated the Tenth Dynasty, Mentuhotep decided to rid the land of the decentralized administration. The kingdom, which was controlled from Thebes, was completely centralized, meaning the governors were stripped of the power they once had. The power was then restored to the hands of the pharaoh.

The Eleventh Dynasty had six more pharaohs after Mentuhotep II. The last king of the Eleventh Dynasty was Mentuhotep IV, who ruled from 1998 BCE to 1991 BCE. Mentuhotep IV sent expeditions to Wadi Hammamat, a dry riverbed in Egypt's Eastern Desert. These expeditions were led by his vizier, Amenemhat, who historians believe became the next pharaoh. It is entirely possible Amenemhat came to power by overthrowing Mentuhotep IV. Still, some archaeologists believe that the rule of Mentuhotep IV collided with Amenemhat I's in the form of a coregency, which would remove usurpation as an option. After ascending to the throne, Amenemhat I founded the Twelfth Dynasty—the ruling dynasty that would bring the true golden age to Egypt. Amenemhat also led a great number of expeditions, similar to his predecessors, in addition to organizing military campaigns in Nubia. He came to the throne in times of turmoil and geopolitical uncertainty, and unfortunately for him, this uncertainty was still present at the end of his reign. Amenemhat was murdered in a conspiracy that his bodyguards executed, and it was a horrible event for his son Senusret I, as described in an ancient Egyptian poem called *Instructions of Amenemhat.* The passage tells about the assassination, written as if Amenemhat is writing about his own murder:

It was after supper, when night had fallen, and I had spent an hour of happiness. I was asleep upon my bed, having become weary, and my heart had begun to follow sleep. When weapons of my counsel were wielded, I had become like a snake of the necropolis. As I came to, I awoke to fighting, and found that it was an attack of the bodyguard. If I had quickly taken weapons in my hand, I would have made the wretches retreat with a charge! But there is none mighty in the night, none who can fight alone; no success will come without a helper. Look, my injury happened while I was without you, when the entourage had not yet heard that I would hand over to you when I had not yet sat with you, that I might make counsels for you; for I did not plan it, I did not foresee it, and my heart had not taken thought of the negligence of servants.

Senusret was campaigning in Libya at the time of his father's assassination, and upon hearing the news, Prince Senusret immediately rushed back to Egypt, where he would take the throne.

Senusret would become one of the most powerful pharaohs of the Twelfth Dynasty, following in his father's footsteps when it came to conquests and expansionist politics. Nubia was still ripe for exploitation, so Senusret sent military expeditions there, and he also established the southern borders of Egypt. The pharaoh himself went on an expedition to an oasis in the Western Desert and established diplomatic relationships with several rulers in the towns of Canaan and Syria. Senusret was succeeded by Amenemhat II, who is thought to be his son. Two generations later, the Middle Kingdom would reach its peak with a warrior king called Senusret III.

Senusret III started his reign in 1878 BCE, and it was marked with conquests and military campaigns. Nubia was still the target of the ruling dynasty, and the pharaoh went on a series of war campaigns there, often leading the battles himself. After finishing his conquests, he built several massive forts to mark the border between the Egyptian kingdom and the conquered parts of Nubia. These forts were manned with scouts, who were supposed to monitor the Medjay, a nomadic Nubian group of people who lived in these parts, and send reports back to the capital. The Medjay were not allowed into the kingdom and beyond the newly established borders; however, trading was allowed between the natives and the Egyptian traders. The reign of Senusret III also records a military campaign in Palestine against Shechem, which was the only war campaign in this region during the Middle Kingdom. The pharaoh also reformed the authority of the kingdom's administration by placing more power into the hands of officials, which could have repeated the scenario of demise and chaos that took place before the Middle Kingdom.

After Senusret III, there were two more generations of pharaohs before the last pharaoh of the Twelfth Dynasty came to the throne. Queen Neferusobek, also known as Sobekneferu, is the first confirmed female Egyptian ruler, although it is believed females ruled as early as the First Dynasty. She was the sister of Amenemhat IV, the penultimate ruler of the Twelfth Dynasty. Since her brother didn't have any male heirs, Neferusobek ascended the throne, reigning from 1806 BCE to 1802 BCE.

By the time Queen Neferusobek left the throne, the golden age of the Middle Kingdom had ended. The rulers who came to power after Neferusobek were somewhat ephemeral and are deceivingly categorized as pharaohs of the Thirteenth Dynasty, even though the pharaohs weren't all related. Many of them were actually commoners. The power was divided again, and chaos reigned, although not to the extent of the period before the Middle Kingdom. After the end of the Thirteenth and Fourteenth Dynasties, the kingdom started to drift from the central authority, and four different dynasties, including a short-lived local dynasty of Abydos, sprung up, separating the power over Egypt. This period is known as the Second Intermediary Period, and it was yet another dark age for the people of Egypt before the kingdom was reborn into the New Kingdom.

The Rise of the Eighteenth Dynasty and the New Kingdom of Egypt: The Egyptian Empire

The New Kingdom began with the Eighteenth Dynasty in 1550 BCE. In this era, Egypt would become a major empire in the ancient Near East and beyond. The entire known civilized world would learn about Egypt and the pharaohs who controlled the lands bathed in the River Nile. The Eighteenth Dynasty was founded by Pharaoh Ahmose I, who was the brother of the last king of the Seventeenth Dynasty. Ahmose I was determined to expel the Hyksos rulers, who had come to Egypt from the Levant and established the Fifteenth Dynasty. Ahmose was succeeded by his son, Amenhotep I, whose reign is obscure due to the lack of written evidence.

His son and successor, Thutmose I, would compensate for his father's lack of action by leading war campaigns. Under his reign, the borders of the kingdom expanded farther than ever before, as Thutmose conquered the Levant and Nubia, entering deep into the territories of these lands. By building the Tombos fortress, the pharaoh expanded the military presence of Egypt in the surrounding regions, which were slowly becoming a part of the empire. Thutmose I was succeeded by his son, Thutmose II, in 1493 BCE. Thutmose II married Hatshepsut, his sister, to better secure his kingship. Thutmose II actually had less right to the throne than his sister-wife since his mother had a lower rank when compared to Hatshepsut's mother, who had royal blood and was closer to the dynastic lineage. During his reign, Thutmose II dealt with rebellions in the Levant and Nubia, as well as defeating a group of nomads called Bedouins. However, Thutmose II wasn't a militaristic man, so his generals won these battles in the name of Egypt.

Hatshepsut, which translates to "The Foremost of Noble Ladies," ascended the throne in 1481 BCE. Her right to the throne was indisputable, as she was the sister, wife, and the daughter of pharaohs, and she had royal blood coursing through her veins. Before her reign, the still undefeated people of Hyksos had destroyed important trading routes in Egypt. So, Hatshepsut turned to rebuilding and reestablishing the trading routes, which was how the wealth of the Eighteenth Dynasty was built. The reign of Hatshepsut is believed to have been peaceful, with only a few or no military campaigns, as she was more focused on expeditions that would bring prosperity to the land. She is still remembered as the first extraordinary woman that history didn't fail to mention.

While his mother focused on bringing economic prosperity to Egypt, her stepson, Thutmose III, was to become a conqueror. He was set on making a true empire out of the kingdom of Egypt, and he succeeded in at least seventeen recorded war campaigns during his reign. After inheriting the throne from his aunt and stepmother in 1479 BCE, the new pharaoh conquered the Niya Kingdom; by doing this, he expanded the borders of Egypt to its greatest extent so far. Since he was the ultimate commander of the Egyptian army, Thutmose III was known as an exceptional warrior, and he used a specific war tactic in his campaigns, which ultimately brought him success. His tactic was to find the weakest link, such as the least defended town, in the chosen kingdom he planned to conquer. Fragment by fragment, and with both patience and might, the pharaoh would defeat the smallest and weakest cities until the enemy kingdom was not able to defend itself.

Thutmose III was succeeded by his son, Amenhotep II, who was also his coregent in the last years of his reign. Although Amenhotep had led several war campaigns and fought for dominance in the Syrian region with Mitanni, Amenemhat, the firstborn of Thutmose III, was supposed to inherit the throne. However, after his untimely death, Amenhotep II was appointed as the pharaoh of Egypt, even though he was born from a lesser wife of Thutmose III, as she wasn't of royal blood.

Next, Thutmose IV came to inherit the power over Egypt, although his older brother was supposed to become the next successor. Although there is no proof, it is presumed that Thutmose IV ousted his brother and then later tried to justify his right to the throne by coming up with a story that was later carved into the Dream Stele. Thutmose IV claimed he fell asleep under the head of the Sphinx, which was buried in the sand. In his dream, the Sphinx told him that he would become the next pharaoh if he restored the beauty and glory of that monument, which he did. Although his right to the throne was considered disputable, Thutmose IV ruled for thirty-nine years. His younger brother, Amenhotep IV, inherited the throne next, eventually changing his name to Akhenaten, meaning "Effective for the Aten."

Monotheism in Egypt with Pharaoh Akhenaten and Queen Nefertiti

Since the very creation of Egypt as a kingdom, the Egyptians believed in polytheism, mainly worshiping Horus and Ra as the holy and sacred unifiers of Upper and Lower Egypt. Akhenaten became known as an enemy in royal archives since he wanted to change the religion to Atenism, a monotheistic religion. Atenism revolved around the god Aten, who represented the sun, much like the god Ra, who had been worshiped for hundreds of years. Egyptian pharaohs had a strong religious cult, as the people believed the rulers of Egypt were actually semi-gods employed by Horus and Ra, among other deities. These deities were represented as life-givers but were also perceived as protectors of the pharaohs in the afterlife. The extent of Akhenaten's religious reforms would haunt him after his death, as all his statues would be removed and hidden by later successors.

Akhenaten married one of the most famous queens in the history of Egypt: Nefertiti. She carried the title of "Great Royal Wife," which meant that she was the primary wife of the pharaoh. Thus, their children would have the utmost advantage when it came to the inheritance of the throne. The queen stood by her husband's side and was described as an idealist, mysterious, and revolutionary but also mad, fanatic, and heretic. The name Nefertiti is translated as "The Beautiful Woman Has Come," and since her origin can't be confirmed, it is suggested that Nefertiti might have arrived from a foreign kingdom as a beauty worthy of a pharaoh. Some evidence suggests that Nefertiti ruled in coregency with her husband in the twelfth year of his reign, which would grant Nefertiti a status that not many queens had. Some archaeologists believe that Nefertiti died of the plague, which came to Egypt with the prisoners of several war campaigns during Akhenaten's rule, while some suggest that she outlived her husband and influenced the next two successors that came to power. Aside from Nefertiti, who is said to have been the pharaoh's greatest love, Akhenaten also married one of his sisters, Meritaten, and his daughter, Mekhetaten, at least according to written evidence. His daughter most likely died due to childbirth at a very young age, either ten or twelve.

Since the Hittites were establishing their dominance in the region, Akhenaten feared that the balance in the ancient Near East would be jeopardized. Allies and vassal territories sought help from the pharaoh, but his peaceful politics hindered those who needed help. Akhenaten wasn't aggressive, and as such, he was not dedicated to military campaigns and battles, even though the geopolitical situation in the region called for such a ruler. The pharaoh's diplomacy skills, however, are praised by some Egyptologists. Akhenaten often focused on internal affairs, as he wanted to strengthen the newly established religion. He commissioned temples and statues that celebrated the god Aten, and he also moved the capital to Amarna, the city he built to honor the glory of Aten. By this point, Nefertiti had yet to ascend the throne in coregency with her husband (if she ever did at all), but the queen still supported the new monotheistic deity.

In 1335 BCE, the throne would be succeeded by Smenkhkare, who continued worshiping Aten. His parentage is also unknown, as historians suggest that Smenkhkare's father may have been Akhenaten or Amenhotep III. Very little is known about this ruler; archaeologists cannot even confirm with certainty whether Smenkhkare was male or female. Since Akhenaten introduced new religious and political views during his reign, it is possible that his heir was a female ruler. Smenkhkare was succeeded shortly after by Neferneferuaten, a name that was used to describe Nefertiti in some inscriptions. This is evidence that shows Nefertiti outlived her husband and ruled as a pharaoh one generation later. It would also explain how the cult of Aten survived two more generations, as the succeeding kings returned to polytheism.

The Rule of Tutankhamun and the End of Amarna

Tutankhamun ascended the throne around 1334 BCE as the last ruler of his family to control the land of Egypt. As the son of Akhenaten, Tutankhamun gained the right to rule even though his mother wasn't the pharaoh's primary wife. Instead, he was born out of the marriage between Akhenaten and one of his sisters. Likewise, Tutankhamun married his own half-sister upon inheriting the throne.

Although his name honors Aten, Tutankhamun decided to reform religion by returning to the old deities and retrieving monuments and rebuilding temples of gods that Egypt never forgot, even during the Amarna period, which refers to when the pharaohs worshiped Aten. Tutankhamun's birth name, Tutankhaten, is translated as the "Living Image of Aten," which signifies that he was born into the reformed religion. However, the name was later changed to "Living Image of Amun" to signify the reform that Tutankhamun himself brought to Egypt. It refers to Amun, a celebrated deity of the Old Kingdom of Egypt.

Tutankhamun was forced to use a cane due to a deformity of his left foot and crippling bone necrosis. Since Tutankhamun was only eight or nine years old when he became the ruler of Egypt, he reigned under the viziership of Ay, who would later become his successor. Tutankhamun and his sister-wife had one stillborn child and one who died shortly after being born, both of which were girls. This left him with no blood-related successors.

Aside from Ay, the pharaoh had other advisors. Horemheb was one of the most notable, as he was Tutankhamun's general. Tutankhamun's father had neglected relationships with allies and neighboring kingdoms, essentially creating a period of economic turmoil. Tutankhamun tried to resolve this with successful diplomatic and war campaigns, and he especially wanted to restore the relationship Egypt had with Mitanni before the reign of Akhenaten. However, it is unlikely that Tutankhamun led any of the war campaigns by himself, as he was severely ill and had major health issues. King Tut, as he is often referred to today, died at the young age of nineteen in 1325 BCE.

After discovering Tutankhamun's intact tomb thousands of years after he was buried and mummified, archaeologists found a serious fracture on his left leg, which might have caused his death in combination with the other health issues he suffered from. A rumor of the pharaoh's curse emerged after the opening of King Tut's tomb, as there were several deaths related to the moving of Tutankhamun's mummy.

Tutankhamun was succeeded by Ay, who only ruled four years before the throne fell into the hands of Horemheb. Horemheb was the last ruler of the Eighteenth Dynasty.

The Peak and End of the New Kingdom – The Warrior Kings

Horemheb didn't have any children, but he did choose someone to inherit his power: his vizier, who took the royal name Ramesses I. Ramesses founded a new dynasty in Egypt, the Nineteenth Dynasty, in 1292 BCE. Ramesses's reign is significant, as he not only founded a new dynasty, but he also brought the New Kingdom to its peak, which continued after his death with his son and grandson.

His son, Seti I, ascended the throne around 1290 BCE, with his name celebrating the god Set (or Seth). Seti's main goal was to reaffirm the old gods that had been worshiped in Egypt before Akhenaten reformed religion during the Amarna period. Seti I also wanted to reestablish control over Canaan and Syria, where the Hittite kingdom was placing great pressure on the sovereignty of Egypt. Seti didn't fear war or battles, so he used any opportunity he had to attack the Hittites. Although he didn't break apart their kingdom, he did retrieve the hegemony over the disputed territories. Seti I also relocated the capital of the kingdom back to Memphis. He accomplished much during his reign, but his glory would be overshadowed by his son and successor, Ramesses II.

Ramesses II became known as Ramesses the Great, and for good reason. The pharaoh is often regarded as the most powerful and most successful ruler of the New Kingdom. In the early years of his reign, Ramesses II started building monuments and temples, as well as rebuilding cities. Later on, he led war campaigns in Nubia, Syria, Libya, and the Levant, and he also reestablished control over Canaan. He prevented havoc from spreading across the Egyptian side of the Mediterranean coast by defeating the Sherden pirates. Ramesses would allow the pirates to attack their intended targets while placing his troops in strategic locations along the coast. He would wait for the pirates to think they had successfully made off with the loot and then attack them, catching the pirates by surprise.

Amid all the battles and campaigns that Ramesses II led during his reign, the pharaoh signed a peace treaty with the Hittite kingdom after the deposed king, Mursili III, fled to the kingdom of Egypt. Ramesses also commissioned a massive temple complex, known as the Ramesseum, and relocated the capital to Thebes, probably because he wanted to be closer to the Egyptian territories in Canaan and Syria. Ramesses II lived for ninety years, and he ruled for an impressive sixty-seven years, the longest of any Egyptian pharaoh. He outlived most of his wives and children and left behind many riches from the conquered lands as his legacy.

After Ramesses's death, his thirteenth son, Merneptah, came to the throne, as his older sons were all dead. The new pharaoh was quite old himself, ruling at the age of seventy years old. Merneptah continued his father's policy, employing the Egyptian army to move against Libya and the Sea Peoples, a mysterious group of seafaring people. However, he could never match the reputation of Ramesses II. He was succeeded by his son Seti II, whose right to the throne was challenged by Amenmesse, who was supposedly his half-brother. Amenmesse usurped control of Thebes and Nubia in Upper Egypt during the fourth year of Seti's reign. Seti II retrieved Upper Egypt back in the fifth year of his reign, removing all statues made in honor of Amenmesse. Amenmesse's remains were desecrated, but the circumstances surrounding his death remain unclear.

Seti's son, Siptah, ascended the throne after his father's death. After his short reign, Twosret succeeded the throne. She was probably Amenmesse's sister and the second wife of Seti II. She died in 1189 BCE, and with her, the New Kingdom and the Nineteenth Dynasty died as well. The kingdom once again entered a period of turmoil and uncertainty. This period was known as the Third Intermediate Period, and it officially lasted from 1133 BCE to 717 BCE, which was when Egypt entered a new era known as the Late Period. During the Third Intermediate Period, Libyan settlers took over the Nile Delta around 1000 BCE, and their autonomy grew stronger. King Piye and the Kushites also took Thebes around 791 BCE. Egypt began its recovery with the Twenty-fifth Dynasty, which oversaw both the Kingdom of Kush and Egypt. Under Pharaoh Taharqa, the empire became as large as the one in the New Kingdom. Other pharaohs from the Twenty-fifth Dynasty worked on restoring buildings, monuments, and cities across the Nile Valley. However, near the end of this period, Egypt's prestige and riches started to decline, as foreign neighbors had fallen under the influence of the Assyrians, who were preparing to invade Egypt. The war between the Assyrians and Egyptians began around 700 BCE during the reigns of Taharqa and his successor, Tantamani. The Assyrians pushed the Kushites back to Nubia, and although Egypt won several battles against the Assyrian forces, the Assyrians occupied Memphis and sacked Thebes.

The Late Period was marked with the rise of a new dynasty, that of the Twenty-sixth Dynasty, also known as the Saite Period. The dynasty was actually formed by Assyrian vassals, who had gained control in Egypt thanks to the Assyrians themselves. The Saite kings turned to Greek mercenaries who had naval forces, as they wished to rid themselves of the Assyrians. Greek influence became evident in Egypt with this turn of events, and the capital was moved to the new city of Sais (hence the name "Saite Period"). Egypt once again enjoyed a thriving economy and culture, but it was only for a brief period of time, as the Persians arrived in 589 BCE, ready to attack and conquer the land of the pharaohs. Egypt wouldn't gain their independence back until 466 BCE, after joining forces with Phoenicia and Cyprus. The Thirtieth Dynasty of Egypt would be the last dynasty with native pharaohs, as the Persians would establish a new dynasty with themselves in charge. Mazaces, the last ruler of the Persian dynasty in Egypt, would hand Egypt over to Alexander the Great without putting up a fight in 332 BCE.

With Alexander the Great, a period of Hellenistic rule commenced in Egypt, known to history as the Ptolemaic dynasty. Alexander the Great was observed as a savior in the eyes of native Egyptians, and he made sure to honor Egyptian traditions and culture after his effortless conquest. This period would last for 300 years before the arrival of the Roman Empire.

Culture, Government, and Military of Egypt

In the ancient world, the government of Egypt was based on the theocratic monarchy. This means the Egyptian pharaohs were appointed by the gods and were intermediaries between the gods and people. The central government was officially established with Pharaoh Narmer and his unification of Upper and Lower Egypt around 3150 BCE. However, historians suggest there was a form of government in Egypt even before this unification. Sources from the Predynastic period also note the existence of monarchs, although it is not known how they operated.

The way the Egyptian government was organized often changed through the centuries. From 3150 BCE to 2890 BCE, the central authority belonged to the pharaoh, while the second-in-command was the vizier. An interesting sidenote about pharaohs is that the term wasn't used until the New Kingdom, although today we refer to all the Egyptian dynastic kings as pharaohs. There were other important government officials as well, such as scribes, tax collectors, and regional governors, and every city had its own mayor. Priests administered temples, which were commissioned by pharaohs in honor of the gods. From 1782 BCE, Egypt would also have a police force as a part of the government.

Egypt's economy was based on agriculture. Low-class peasants would farm the lands that belonged to landowners. Some of the crops and produce were kept by the peasants, while a greater portion was given to the landowners. Landowners would give some of the produce to the government, which the king would use for trading purposes. The king would personally control the wealth of the kingdom, traveling across the districts to assess their riches rather than believing the regional governors. That way, the pharaohs also demonstrated their presence and power to the people. Tax collectors would inspect each province and district after the king and take a certain amount of goods, which was given to the central government. By the end of the Old Kingdom, this type of government was slowly crumbling, as provincial governors had been given greater authority with the decentralization of the government. And as they were getting richer, they cared less about the pharaoh's authority. This change might have led to the collapse of the Old Kingdom in combination with other malevolent circumstances.

Egypt started using official military units in the Old Kingdom around 2686 BCE; however, a military hierarchy wasn't established until the Middle Kingdom around 2055 BCE. By the time the New Kingdom was formed around 1550 BCE, the Egyptian military was divided into three branches: the infantry, the chariotry, and the naval forces. The army was divided into two parts, located in the north and the south, and these armies would be further divided into four. The four armies would be named after the gods Ptah, Sutekh, Ra, and Amen. Mercenaries were also used in times of war with the native Egyptian army. Captains would usually be lower-ranked princes of noble houses or highly educated officials with strong political or educational backgrounds who were chosen by army commanders. Egyptian armies also used projectile weapons in combat, such as slings, javelins, spears, and throwing sticks.

The administration wouldn't haven't even existed if it wasn't for literacy. The Egyptian language was an Afro-Asiatic language, and it was spoken within the territories of the ancient Egyptian kingdom. The earliest stage of the language was attested in 3300 BCE, at a time when hieroglyphs weren't fully developed. The most extensive texts date as far back as the Old Kingdom, and they were written on the walls of pyramids, tombs, and temples across Egypt. Aside from writing on walls and clay tablets, Egyptians used papyrus, a form of thick paper dating from the Old Kingdom. Papyrus was perishable, so many Egyptian texts are believed to have been lost.

Chapter 8 – The Middle and New Kingdoms of the Hittite: The Dark Ages and the Glory of the Hittite Empire

The Old Hittite Kingdom ended around the mid-15th century BCE with the reign of Tahurwaili. The end of the Old Kingdom introduced a new era known as the Middle Kingdom, which corresponds to the Hittite Kingdom's dark ages. This period was brief and is obscure, as not many surviving records of the Middle Kingdom survived, for the Hittites were constantly weakened by attacks. The kingdom mainly suffered attacks from the Kaska, who arrived from the shores of the Black Sea.

Telipinu was the last ruler of the Old Kingdom, and he was succeeded by Tahurwaili. This happened in the mid-15th century, but the exact date is not known. Tahurwaili was Telipinu's first cousin, which made him the direct successor to the throne, as Telipinu had no sons who could inherit his position. Telipinu had previously exiled Alluwamna, his son-in-law; however, Alluwamna returned after his death to take over the throne. It is not known if he ruled before Tahurwaili or after, but it is believed he ruled very briefly.

The next king of the Middle Kingdom was Hantili II. He was the son of Harapseki, Telipinu's daughter, and King Alluwamna. As with other kings in the Middle Kingdom, little is known about Hantili's reign, including when he succeeded the throne. Hantili II was succeeded by Zidanta II, who was probably his nephew. Zidanta II ascended the throne in 1450 BCE and probably ruled until 1440 BCE. Huzziya II followed; however, the relation between the two kings, the date of his accession to the throne, and the length of his reign is not known. What is known is that Huzziya II was killed by his own royal bodyguard, Muwatalli. Muwatalli I may have even been Huzziya's brother, which might have facilitated his right to the throne.

Muwatalli I's reign was also violently interrupted, as he was killed by Kantuzili, who was the overseer of the Gold Chariot Fighters, and Himuili, the chief of the royal servants. Muwa, who was the chief of the royal bodyguard and probably the brother of Muwatalli, fled the kingdom and asked for help from the Hurrians, possibly to get to the throne. In the meantime, one of the king's assassins, Kantuzili, joined forces with Tudhaliya. The Hurrians agreed to help Muwa, although the terms of the agreement remain unknown. Muwa and the Hurrians clashed with Kantuzili and Tudhaliya. The latter won, and the Hurrians were pushed back. This is how Tudhaliya came to the throne around 1430 BCE. Tudhaliya might have been a grandson of Huzziya II, a Middle Kingdom ruler, making him the direct successor to Muwattalli I. However, as with many other rulers, it is not known for sure how Tudhaliya was related to the king.

This victory helped Tudhaliya reconfigure the alliance with Syria and also led the Yamhad king to change sides and provide support to Tudhaliya. Such political change didn't last long, as Halab (the capital of Yamhad) was once again conquered by the Hurrians. That didn't stop Tudhaliya from expanding the borders of his kingdom to the far eastern parts of Anatolia. He made Zippasla a vassal territory of the

Hittites and conquered Assuwa, which was a confederation of twenty-two Anatolian city-states created sometime before 1400 BCE. Some historians consider Tudhaliya I to be the first king of the New Kingdom. However, other scholars think this honor belongs to King Suppiluliuma I, who will be mentioned later in the chapter. It is more likely that Tudhaliya I was the first king of the New Kingdom, as the Hittite kingdom slowly recovered from the period known as the dark ages.

The Legacy of Tudhaliya I: The New Kingdom and the Rise of the Hittite Empire

One of the most important legacies that the kings of the dark ages left to their successors was their ability to make treaties and alliances with the neighboring lands. The Hittite settlements were slowly forming into an empire, which is why the New Kingdom is also known as the Hittite Empire period. The Hittites started to make settlements in southern Anatolia, making treaties to establish their presence and expand their growing empire. The king started to be referred by the citizens as "My Sun," as the kingship was gaining strength.

Tudhaliya I was succeeded by his son-in-law, Arnuwanda I. Arnuwanda ruled in coregency with Tudhaliya in the early 14th century BCE. Arnuwanda I had two sons, Asmi-Sarruma and Tudhaliya, who became the next king in 1422 BCE. Tudhaliya II was nothing like Tudhaliya I, as he wasn't very successful in keeping the empire intact. During his reign, he lost a part of the conquered territories in Anatolia, and the capital of the Hittite kingdom burned to the ground. He was succeeded by Tudhaliya III, who may not have even ruled, as there are no dates or records attesting his reign. The supposed king Tudhaliya III was killed by a group of officers in a conspiracy. His successor, Suppiluliuma, who was most likely his brother, was involved in the assassination. Suppiluliuma I ascended the throne in 1408 BCE and ruled until 1386 BCE. As mentioned above, some historians believe the New Kingdom started with Suppiluliuma I. This is because Suppiluliuma turned out to be a warrior king and a successful statesman, who even dared to challenge the Egyptian empire. Before he became the king, Suppiluliuma I was the army general and the chief advisor of Tudhaliya II. Suppiluliuma knew the importance of diplomatic relationships, so he married a sister of the Hayasan king and married his own daughter off to Maskhuiluwa, the ruler of the Arzawan state of Mira. The king also married a Babylonian princess. Suppiluliuma reconquered some of the Arzawan territories and defeated the Mitanni kingdom, which was reduced to a small city-state.

Although his victory over the Mitanni kingdom testified his military glory, Suppiluliuma I made his mark by taking advantage of the situation in Egypt during the period of Amarna and the reign of Pharaoh Akhenaten. Akhenaten's rule brought serious religious reforms and turmoil to Egypt, and Suppiluliuma took advantage of this by conquering the Egyptian territory in Syria. This conquest caused many of the Egyptian vassals to revolt. Although Suppiluliuma was victorious in war, he didn't neglect the need for diplomacy and alliances. He decided to send a letter to the widow of Tutankhamun, asking her to marry one of his sons, who would then rule with her as the Egyptian pharaoh. Dakhamunzu, King Tut's widow, agreed to this, so Suppiluliuma sent Prince Zannanza to Egypt. Unfortunately, Zannanza never made it to Egypt. He died on his way there, so Suppiluliuma assumed that Pharaoh Ay, who had seized the throne of Egypt in the meantime, had something to do with his son's death. That was the main motive behind the war between the Hittites and Egyptians. Angry that he wasn't able to secure the Egyptian throne or gain closure for his son's death, Suppiluliuma unleashed his army on the vassal states of Egypt in northern Syria and Canaan. Victorious King Suppiluliuma brought many Egyptian prisoners to his kingdom.

What Suppiluliuma didn't know was that the prisoners he took back home would be his demise. The prisoners were infected with the plague, which ravaged the Hittite kingdom, killing Suppiluliuma and his successor, Arnuwanda II. He came to the throne after his father's death in 1386 BCE, but he died only a year later. He was succeeded by Mursili II, his brother, who was the next in line to inherit the throne. Mursili II was the king of Hittites until 1359 BCE.

The Hittites had many enemies. During this period, the most notable were the Arzawan kingdom and the Kaska. According to Mursili's annals, his enemies considered him to be a child and an inexperienced king, who only came to the throne because of the sudden death of his brother. However, despite the scorn of his enemies, Mursili II turned out to be an adequate statesman, as he was able to secure the territory of his kingdom. He successfully stopped the invasion of the Kaska, all while securing the northern borders of the kingdom. The Arzawan king, Uhhaziti, threatened the Hittites from the west, and he tried to win over some of the Hittite allies, but Mursili managed to put these efforts down. Although he was probably unprepared for the throne, Mursili II was a successful ruler. He was succeeded by his son, Muwatalli II, after his death in 1359 BCE.

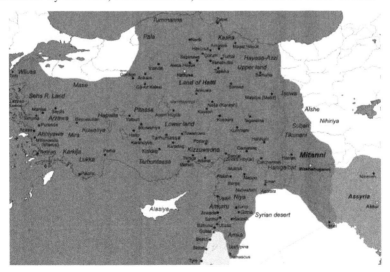

The Hittite Empire at its greatest extent under the reign of Suppiluliuma I

(https://images.app.goo.gl/8kvuf3AtBg5abjSv6)

Muwatalli II changed the capital of Hattusa to Tarhuntassa, whose exact location remains unknown. Scholars believe the king moved the capital farther south because Hattusa bordered the Kaska. Muwatalli II is best known for his role in the Battle of Kadesh, which took place sometime around 1338 BCE. It was fought against Egypt, which was ruled by Ramesses II, who was seeking to reclaim territory the Hittites had taken. Muwatalli II first sent his scouts to find the exact location of the Egyptian troops, as he knew they were approaching the Hittite lands. The scouts found the Egyptians when they were nearing Kadesh, and they pretended to be deserters from the Hittite army. The scouts told Ramesses's men that Muwatalli's troops were far away in Aleppo, which was hundreds of miles from Kadesh. Soon afterward, several other Hittite scouts were caught, and Ramesses II then figured out what was going on. Muwatalli wasn't near Aleppo; he was right outside of Kadesh with his troops, ready to attack. Muwatalli didn't waste any time attacking the Egyptian troops outside of Kadesh. Ramesses II had only one of his two divisions, as the second had yet to arrive. Muwatalli took advantage of this. While he directly attacked the first division, he also sent charioteers to attack Ramesses's camp. Ramesses managed to fend off the attack, which he saw as a victory, proclaiming that he won the battle the next day. However, Muwatalli's records show that he also proclaimed victory over Ramesses and the Egyptians. Although both sides claimed victory, historians believe they both suffered great losses and that the battle led to a reduction of military power.

In 1336 BCE, Muwatalli II died, and he was succeeded by his eldest surviving son, Mursili III, who would rule until 1329 BCE. Mursili III decided to move the capital back to Hattusa. After this move, Mursili lost Hanigalbat in northern Syria to the Assyrians, which consequently weakened his legitimacy as a ruler. In the seventh year of his reign, Mursili III realized his uncle Hattusili was a threat to his reign, as he was a powerful man with a connection to the throne. To deal with this problem, Mursili attacked his uncle's strongholds in Nerik and Hakpissa, which were a part of the kingdom's borders.

Hattusili wrote about the way he was affected by his nephew's attack, stating that after serving the crown for seven years, he would no longer submit to the king. According to Hattusili, if Mursili had never taken his fortress in Hakpissa from him, Hattusili would never have started a war to challenge the throne. It appears Mursili created a scenario for his own demise by fearing the power of his uncle. Hattusili gathered a sufficient military force to remove his nephew from the throne. He was known throughout the kingdom for his participation in the Battle of Kadesh, and he recruited allies from the strongholds that had been taken by his nephew. Hattusili's forces even included the Kaska, who were enemies of the Hittites. Thanks to his experience in military strategy and his allied forces, Hattusili was able to seize the throne from his nephew. Mursili wasn't killed, and he fled to Egypt, yet another enemy of the Hittite, to attempt to convince Ramesses II to help him retrieve his throne back. The newly crowned Hattusili III wrote to the pharaoh, asking him to extradite his nephew. The two forces were once again close to starting another war, but thankfully, a treaty between Egypt and the Hittite kingdom was established. The treaty also contained a clause of extradition, after which all traces of Mursili III are lost. Some evidence suggests Mursili was banished by Hattusili III to the land of Nuhasse, where he was given fortified towns on the edge of the empire to watch over.

Hattusili III the War King and the Demise of the Hittite Empire

When Hattusili III usurped the throne, driven by anger and disappointment in his nephew, he was immediately faced with problems concerning the dominance of the kingdom over the vassal lands in the west. The vassals had sworn to the Hittite king to attack any usurper, which Hattusili III was. Thus, the vassals found themselves in an uncertain situation. Every vassal state could technically attack Hattusili under the excuse of attacking the usurper and defending the interests of the Hittite kingdom. Ahhiyawa, in western Anatolia, might have been the greatest threat, as it rivaled the Hittites. This vassal state had sided with King Mursili III, but they did not actually help him in the civil war against Hattusili III. Ahhiyawa was slowly taking control over some of the Hittite allies, which included the Lukka lands in the far south of Anatolia.

Hattusili III knew he ascended the throne in an uncommon way. Although assassination was a fairly common way of inheriting the throne in the Hittite Empire, Hattusili III was the first king to use an army to gain power. Hattusili wanted to justify his deeds, which he tried by writing his version of the story in what is known as *The Apology*. The king explains how Mursili did him wrong, which made him rebel against him. He emphasizes that no one got hurt and that his motive was to unify the kingdom.

Once he affirmed his rule as the "Great King," Hattusili decided to upgrade the palace of Buyukkale by completely rebuilding the citadel's platform, creating three gates at the southern peak of the palace. Despite affirming his right to the throne, Hattusili III was soon faced with a major threat coming from the west: the vassal kings. The Lukka warriors decided to take advantage of the oath they had made to Mursili to attack the Hittite kingdom. The Lukka warriors arrived at the Hulaya River Land (an unknown area in western Anatolia), where another district of the kingdom, centered in the city of Hawaliya, revolted against the Hittite usurper. Other cities, whose names are not well preserved, also revolted in the western part of the kingdom, challenging Hattusili's potential to preserve the kingdom's borders. Hattusili couldn't control these incursions, which led to more attacks from other enemies. The city of Millawanda, with Piyama-radu at its head, invaded the Hittite lands. Hattusili III sent a messenger to Piyama-radu, questioning his deeds and urging him to stop. It seems Hattusili's message didn't have a particularly strong impact on Piyama-radu. Instead, it showed weakness. If Hattusili couldn't handle the first wave of attacks by the vassals, then it wouldn't take much to break him. Piyama-radu went on to conquer the entire Hulaya River Land

and a part of the Lower Land (today's Turkey). He even arrived at the land of Nahita, located in the east of the kingdom. Hattusili needed to act and take back control over these territories. He made a good start by regaining the Hulaya River Land and a great part of the Lower Land, even though it seems he didn't reestablish his control in the coastal territories. Hattusili needed to find a way to regain control over the vassal kingdoms, so he decided to make a vassal out of Tarhuntassa, where the capital had been under Muwatalli II. Hattusili created a new kingdom there and placed his nephew, Ulmi-Tessup, the son of Muwatalli II, as the king. The new king of Tarhuntassa was encouraged to reclaim the lost territories with his own resources, as specified by a treaty created between Ulmi-Tessup and Hattusili. It was expected of Ulmi-Tessup to expand his dominance to the southern and southwestern borders of the kingdom, and he did not fail this task. By the end of Hattusili's reign, the territory of Tarhuntassa would be expanded to the Kastaraya River (Asku River) in the west and the Mediterranean Sea in the south.

As the imperial strength of Hattusili's kingdom grew, he could focus on building and maintaining relations with neighboring kingdoms. One of the most important treaties made by Hattusili III was with Egyptian Pharaoh Ramesses II. This was known as the Eternal Treaty or as the Treaty of Kadesh. Although the Treaty of Kadesh is one of its names, this treaty was signed fifteen years after the battle. Relations between Ramesses and Hattusili were fairly close, as the pharaoh and king frequently exchanged correspondence. In fact, the idea for Ramesses to marry Hattusili's daughter emerged from this correspondence. Hattusili promised to give a great dowry ("greater than the dowry of a Babylonian princess"), telling the pharaoh that his daughter would bring servants, cattle, horses, and sheep to the land of Aya, which was the border of the Hittite kingdom. However, Hattusili's daughter was delayed from making her journey, as Hattusili had troubles with collecting everything for the dowry. Hattusili's daughter finally arrived in Egypt in around the thirty-fourth year of Ramesses's reign, but she still married the pharaoh. Soon afterward,

Hattusili married another daughter to the elderly pharaoh. Diplomatic relations continued, and Egypt even sent grain to the Hittite kingdom to resolve the problem of famine. These friendly relations continued even during the reign of Hattusili's successor, his youngest son, Tudhaliya IV, who came to the throne in 1301 BCE. Hattusili and Tudhaliya ruled together in a coregency for the first years of Tudhaliya's reign.

In 1273 BCE, Tudhaliya died, and the throne was succeeded by his son, Arnuwanda III. Arnuwanda only ruled for two years and was succeeded by his brother, Suppiluliuma II. He was the last king of the New Kingdom era. Suppiluliuma II ruled from 1271 BCE to 1242 BCE. A year before he became king, in 1272 BCE, Suppiluliuma commanded a fleet against the Cypriots, who came from Cyprus. This is the first recorded naval battle in history. During Suppiluliuma's reign, the Sea Peoples invaded the Hittite kingdom, first taking Cyprus and Cilicia, then cutting off the Hittite trade routes. The capital of Hattusa was burnt to the ground, which marked the end of Suppiluliuma's reign and the end of the Hittite Empire. Some claim the king "vanished," while some believe he was killed in the chaos. The Kaska most likely moved in to take over the region.

Culture, Military, and Government of the Hittite Kingdom

According to scholars, the Hittites might have had the first constitutional monarchy when they transitioned to the New Kingdom. In the Old Kingdom, kings had too much power and ruled as absolute monarchs. The king was the only entity in the kingdom who had the right to make decisions and rule as he pleased. In the New Kingdom, the king's power could be constrained to some extent, as the *pankus* (a general assembly) would take care of the kingdom's legal matters and were utilized for other decisions as well, such as helping the king pick his successor. The Hittites didn't establish a clear line of succession, which is how the youngest son could inherit the throne even if the eldest son was alive and able to succeed. That is perhaps why assassinations were so common. The *pankus* also had judicial duties. The law of the Hittites was well established, and it even recognized the difference between accidental and intentional law breaches.

The Hittite culture was greatly influenced by neighboring kingdoms throughout their history, such as the Egyptians, Akkadians, and Hatti, so their clothes and art often resembled these civilizations. The language of the Hittites belonged to the family of Anatolian Indo-European languages, and they used Hittite cuneiform and Luwian hieroglyphs for writing.

The Hittite Empire would have never taken the true form of an imperialistic force if it weren't for weapons and warfare. In the Battle of Kadesh, King Muwatalli II led an army that numbered between 17,000 and 20,000 men. The fact that Muwatalli managed to gather such a large force is supported by the king's ability to utilize and employ the manpower provided by vassal kingdoms and city-states. The army had archers, infantry, and chariots. The Hittite infantry used medium-length spears, axes, and sickle swords, and they were equipped with scale armor, helmets, and leather boots. The most noticeable part of their equipment was the shield, which was designed in the form of the number eight. The thin waist of the shield made it light enough to carry while still offering solid protection. The chariotry in the Hittite army was the decision-making unit, as this unit was the first to attack.

Chapter 9 –Beyond the Wars and Thrones: The Everyday Life of Common People in the Ancient Near East

The history of the ancient Neat East goes beyond the wars for succession and battles for territory. To really get an insight into the ancient Near East, one must ask about the everyday life of the common people. Different civilizations had different ways of life and habits, and these civilizations often clashed and assimilated with one another to a certain extent.

Everyday Life in Mesopotamia

There were not many distinct social classes in ancient Mesopotamia. There were the wealthy and the poor. The official classes were the royals, nobility, priests and priestesses, upper class, lower class, and slaves. A poor Mesopotamian would begin his day with the women in the house preparing breakfast, which could have been soup, porridge, or bread with beer. In the homes of the rich and wealthy, servants prepared breakfast, which could have contained fruit and nuts alongside staple foods such as beer, bread, onions, and porridge made out of different types of grains, such as barley and wheat. There were usually two meals, one in the morning before work and another in the evening after work. Sometimes, Mesopotamians would bring some bread and beer as a snack to work to replenish themselves during the day. On special occasions, they cooked meat—mostly lamb.

Most women took care of their families and stayed home as homesteaders; however, some women worked as bakers, potters, tavern keepers, and weavers. Men worked in a variety of occupations, including farming, construction work, jewelry making, goldsmithing, and carpentry. Men could also work as musicians, tavern owners, metallurgists, artists, basket makers, and brick makers. Women and men alike could also become prostitutes. Professions like perfume markers, jewelry makers, and prostitutes could be considered elite jobs in cases of exceptional skill and being in favor of the king. Interestingly, women were the first doctors and dentists, as well as the first tavern keepers and brewers in ancient Mesopotamia. However, these professions were soon dominated by men, as they proved to be lucrative occupations.

The everyday life of Mesopotamians was greatly influenced by religion. They offered sacrifices to the gods before and after erecting buildings and temples, as well as daily and before meals.

Homes were usually built out of mud bricks. Poor citizens lived in buildings with several stories, usually in narrow streets far from the city center, and with no windows. They used to sleep on their roofs during hot days, as there was no other way to cool down from the high temperatures. Wealthy people lived closer to the palace in the center of the city and usually in houses with gardens. They had servants and windows for extra light and fresh air. They also used sesame oil lamps, while the poor went to bed when it became dark to save on oil or due to the lack of lamps altogether. Interestingly, even though there were strictly defined social classes, the lower class could earn their way and become upper-class citizens.

Slaves could buy their freedom and weren't only used for manual labor. They could also be tutors, accountants, or jewelry makers. They could even manage the estates of the wealthy. One could become a slave if they were kidnapped, sold to pay off their family's debt or their own debt, or as a punishment for a crime.

Everyday Life in Ancient Egypt

In ancient Egypt, slaves, servants, and farmers working on the estates of the king and nobility were at the bottom of the social class pyramid. The middle-class status belonged to soldiers, builders working on temples and royal buildings, artists, and sailors. Above this class were the scribes, accountants, and doctors, who enjoyed great respect in Egypt. They were followed by the upper class—the nobility. At the top of the social pyramid was the royal family, who were considered to be immortal and in direct contact with the gods.

Magic was a great part of everyday life in ancient Egypt, as it was believed the gods acted through a divine, somewhat magical force. Egyptians believed in balance, which is why everyone was encouraged to live in peace, as it would bring about prosperity. The Egyptians enjoyed festivals and festivities, and spending time with family and friends was very important to them. They also enjoyed sports, reading, and games.

Rich or poor, an Egyptian would be considered incomplete if they remained unmarried. Boys were advised to marry at a young age and have as many children as possible. Sons usually inherited their professions from their fathers, and they would spend much time together so the son would be well prepared when he entered the workforce. Cooking, cleaning, and caring for the children were greatly appreciated skills of which women were in charge. Egyptian art depicts women as pale caretakers staying at home to provide for the home and children, while the men are painted with darker skin, indicating they would have spent more time outside working. Women had the same rights as men and were allowed to own property by themselves and without a male legal guardian.

Ancient Egyptians mostly lived in prosperity regardless of their social class, although slaves lived in more modest conditions and had restricted rights. This was probably why Egyptians believed the afterlife was a continuation of life on earth. Ancient Egyptians lived in a fertile land, so they had food and water in abundance. A common family would enjoy fish, vegetables, fruit, bread, and grain on a regular basis, as well as the occasional small game. The nobility and upper class ate more meat on a regular basis; however, food wasn't lacking in any social class. Everyone drank beer and wine was present only in the homes of the rich and wealthy, which included the royal family. Egyptians wore simple garments, although the royals had more "festive" white pleated garments. Common Egyptians wore clothes made of linen, shawls, and woven sandals. They would patch their garments until they were no longer wearable. When that happened, these garments would be used as mummy wraps.

Thanks to mummification, doctors of ancient Egypt could learn more about the human body, but they still didn't understand how exactly the human body works. They believed the body was comprised of a series of canals, such as nerves and veins, that all led to the center of the body—the heart. If any of these canals flooded, Egyptian doctors believed it was the cause of some illness. They would often pierce holes in the aching parts of the body, hoping to unclog these canals and remove the source of the illness. Still, Egyptian doctors were considered to be the best in the Mediterranean, combining magic and rituals with medicinal knowledge and diagnoses.

The royals, nobility, and court officials all lived in prosperity. Scribes also enjoyed a comfortable lifestyle, as it was believed they were chosen by the gods to record events through the written word. All priests and physicians were scribes, but not all scribes were involved in those fields. Men and women alike could become physicians and scribes by getting a higher education. However, these professions were predominantly male occupations.

Lower-class peasants were mostly farmers, who had small private gardens that their wives tended to while they were working the noblemen's fields. They kept some of the crops for themselves as compensation for their labor, and the rest was given to the landowners. The lowest social class with the least amenities were the slaves. Slaves were usually people who had broken the law, had to pay a debt, or were foreigners captured in war. Slaves could gain their freedom after paying their debts or performing a labor sentence.

Everyday Life in the Hittite Kingdom

If you lived in the Hittite kingdom around 3,500 years ago in the area of central Anatolia, chances are you would have been an ethnic mixture of Luwian, Hurrian, Hittite, and Hattian, maybe even Greek and Canaanite. The mortality rate of children was high, so any parent was lucky to see their child survive past the age of five. Many families had more than six to seven children, especially upper-class families, as they could afford physicians and good medical care for their infants. Girls and boys were welcomed to the world equally and given female, male, or gender-neutral names. Youngsters would begin to learn and train for their profession at the age of seven, usually learning their family craft. Common boys would typically learn how to farm or make pottery, while girls learned from their mothers how to cook and weave. Children would also learn to write cuneiform letters for hours.

Women are depicted in ancient Hittite art with long dark hair, and men are shown with shoulder-length hair and a perfectly shaved face. Men wore kilts with tunics and belts made of leather, while women wore long dresses. All clothes were either made of wool or linen. Married women would also wear veils. The Hittites dyed their clothes, using blue, red, white, green, black, and yellow. The wealthy could show off their affluence with purple dye, which was imported from Lesbos or the Levant, and wore jewelry.

The kingdom was often raided on the outskirts, so one would consider themselves lucky if they lived in the heart of the kingdom. The majority of people lived in small villages surrounded by trees and thick forests. As in Mesopotamia, people often ate before work and after work, while some brought snacks to work, like bread and beer. Bread was usually made out of barley and wheat, but it could also be made out of lentils and beans. The Hittites ate moon bread, spear bread, fig bread, flatbread, and honey bread. Honey was a common food in the kingdom. The diet of an average Hittite would include dairy products, vegetables, fruit, and meat. Commoners of the Hittite kingdom might have eaten meat more often than commoners in the neighboring civilizations of Egypt and Mesopotamia. They ate peas, cucumber, carrots, leek, dates, onion, garlic, grapes, pomegranate, beans, olives, lentils, milk, butter, and cheese. The popular types of meat were goat, sheep, cow, and sometimes wild game. Many dishes were flavored with cumin and coriander, and some of the most popular meals were porridge and stews with meat and veggies. The Hittites drank water, milk, beer, and wine, and they even had a drink that was a combination of wine and beer.

There were three distinctive social classes: upper, lower, and slaves. The upper class included royals, the nobility, court officials, and people with lucrative occupations. Upper-class men were district leaders, and they worked and lived in the royal court or owned property. The lower class was mostly comprised of peasants. Slaves were considered to be the lowest social class, and they had little to no freedom to make their own choices. Slaves were made through conquests and punishments, as in other cultures of the ancient Near East.

Everyday Life in Hammurabi's Babylon

Hammurabi's Babylon was probably one of the most beautiful cities in the ancient Near East. Hammurabi wanted to honor the patron god Marduk with a glorious city proportionate to the power of this deity.

At the time, every city in the Babylonian Empire had its own patron deity, and the center of the empire, Babylon, was protected by Marduk. The city had tall, strong walls framed with rich greenery. The summers were hot and dry, so people spent time on the rooftops in the evening and in the mornings to try and get some refreshing breeze. They even slept and cooked on the roofs. The wealthier could afford sheltered roofs with four walls to create a shade from the sun, and they usually cultivated grape arbors for food. Even the poorest in the city had three levels of living space. The rooftop was perhaps the most important level of the house. Each house had a small or large garden, where women kept poultry, sheep, or a few goats, alongside with cultivating fruit and vegetables.

The city had tall walls and narrow streets, and everyone's front doors were accessible from the street. The streets were used for garbage as well. People used to just throw their trash away in the streets, in front of their homes. The smell was probably horrific, and this problem would be solved from time to time by having a layer of clay added across the city's streets. As a consequence, the level of streets became higher, which called for stairs leading down to the front doors.

The Hanging Gardens, one of the Seven Wonders of the Ancient World, were in Babylon, although it is not known for certain if they even existed at all. It is believed to have been created by Nebuchadnezzar II, who wanted to make something beautiful for his wife, as she was homesick. In the center of the city stood a stele with Hammurabi's law engraved in stone. This stele provided laws that had to be honored to keep the balance in the crowded but peaceful city.

With proper law regulations came prosperity, and Babylon thrived. Soon, it became a major trading center, and people could buy anything from coats and jewelry to cheese, milk, fish, meat, and fresh vegetables and fruit. Date wine was one of the most popular drinks in Babylon. Bread was the main staple food in the city and the Babylonian Empire in general.

According to the Babylonian law code, there were three distinctive social classes: *Awilu* (the upper class, i.e., nobility), *Mushkenu* (the lower class), and *Wardu* (the slaves). Unlike in Egypt and the Hittite kingdom, women and men weren't treated equally, and the law prescribed different punishments depending on the perpetrator's gender.

Chapter 10 – The Birth of Religions in the Ancient Near East: The Cradle of Civilization and the Gods

The Fertile Crescent wasn't only the Cradle of Civilization. It was also the birthplace of religions that are still alive today, with gods who are still worshipped. Wars, hunger, droughts, floods, death, the sun, the moon, night, and day—all of these experiences, events, and natural phenomena needed to be explained, and the origin of these things was often identified as the will of the gods or a manifestation of the gods themselves.

Polytheism was deeply rooted in the lands and civilizations of the Fertile Crescent. The Assyrians and Babylonians believed that the gods were protectors of humankind. Still, these deities were believed to be capable of anger as well. Ancient civilizations believed that if something bad happened to them—for instance, war, famine, or drought—they must have done something to anger the gods.

Religions in Mesopotamia

The Mesopotamians had hundreds of gods and deity cults, as there were different deities for every profession and every city. The gods who protected the Mesopotamian cities were considered patron deities, and there were also major gods who controlled important realms of life in the ancient world, such as the sky, the sun, and the air.

Anu was the father and creator of all gods, and he was the god of the sky, from where he ruled over the universe. Utu was the god of the sun and also the facilitator of justice and truth. Other major deities were Enlil, the god of the air; Inanna, the goddess of love and war; Nanna, the god of the moon; Enki, the god of freshwater, magic, and wisdom; and Ninhursag, the goddess of the earth. The major deities were worshipped by the kings, while the commoners of Mesopotamia paid more attention to personal gods, who they considered their guardian angels. Kings would show their devotion to the major deities by commissioning temples, and each temple had its own deity.

The civilizations of Akkad, Sumer, and Assyria shared some of their religious beliefs and mythology, although there were minor changes in the story of Earth's creation and the births of the gods and their names.

Religions in Ancient Iran

The cultures of ancient Iran had many different spiritual beliefs and religions, which included Yazdanism, Mandeanism, and Zoroastrianism, among others. The people of Mitanni, who came into conflict with the ancient Egyptians on several occasions, practiced Zoroastrianism, which is one of the world's oldest continuously practiced religions. Zoroastrianism was founded by the spiritual leader Zoroaster, who is also known as Zarathustra. His central writings are contained in the Avesta, which is a compilation of religious texts. The main deity is Ahura Mazda, translated as the "Wise Lord." Ahura

Mazda is proclaimed to be the supreme creator of the universe, and he is divided into three: the earth, atmosphere, and heaven. The opposite of the Wise Lord would be Angra Mainyu ("evil thought"), who is actually the embodiment of a destructive spirit. Ahura Mazda gave people free will so they could choose whether to worship the Wise Lord or give in to the influence of Angra Mainyu. This religion tells a story about the world of good and evil, combined with the ideology that good will always prevail.

Religions in Anatolia

Before Judaism, Christianity, and Islam were formed as major religions in Asia and Europe, Mesopotamian mythology and polytheistic religion dominated Anatolia. The civilizations of Akkad, Sumer, and Assyria shared some of their religious beliefs and mythology, although there were minor changes in the story of Earth's creation and the births of the gods and their names. The Hittites also used some elements from Mesopotamian religion, combined with the Proto-Indo-European religion. Proto-Indo-European religion represents a collection of mythology that includes Greek, Roman, Slavic, Celtic, Baltic, and even Hittite. There are many similarities between the mythologies of civilizations, especially regarding creation, the underworld (otherworld), life after death, and the main deities. The spiritual beliefs of the Hittites were also influenced by the Hurrians, a neighboring civilization. The mythology and religion of the Hittites remain incomplete to this day, as not all religious scriptures survived the ravages of time. What is known today about their religion is that deities were commonly shown on the backs of different animals, while some gods were shown as animals. Hittites worshipped their gods through Huwasi stones, which were considered to be sacred and were placed in temples or among trees and plants. Two main Hittite deities known to history are the God-Sun and the God-Storm. Moreover, the Hittite kingdom was known as the kingdom of a thousand gods, as their religion assimilated with the Mesopotamians, Hurrians, Canaanites, and Hattians.

Religions in the Levant

In the Levant, the dominant religions were Yahwism and the religion of the ancient Canaanite people. Yahwism, a monolatristic religion, dates back to the Late Bronze Age or the Early Iron Age. Yahwism was considered to be related to the Canaanite culture until Yahwism separated its spiritual identity from the supposed Canaanite heritage thousands of years later in the 6th century BCE. Yahweh began as a deity in control of wars and storms. He was in control of a heavenly army as well, leading his sacred warriors to battles against the enemies of the Israelite kingdom. Yahweh was worshipped with a number of other gods and goddesses, who all signified different phenomena, local protection, professions, and celestial bodies, similar to the religion in Mesopotamia or Egypt. It is unclear when Yahwism arrived in the Levant, although it is presumed this religion might have been attested in the early 11th century BCE. The Canaanite gods were worshipped alongside Yahweh for centuries—for at least 500 years—while Yahweh became the national deity of the Israelite kingdoms in the Iron Age.

The Canaanite religion is considered to be one of the earliest forms of ancient Semitic religions, and it represented a complex line of deities who were related to each other. They ruled the humans and the skies. El and Asherah were the primary deities. The literal meaning of El is "deity" or "god," and he was the father of the other gods. Asherah was the mother goddess and is also mentioned in writings of the Hittites and Akkadians. The Canaanite religion may also be categorized as a monolatristic religion, as it consistently prescribes worshiping a single deity while recognizing that other gods and goddesses also exist. While the Canaanite religion is not the same as Yahwism, Yahwism evolved from the Canaanite religion, later on transforming into Judaism. The transformation of these religions is unclear, but it may have started with prophecies and religious amendments made by Prophets Elijah, Josiah, and Hezekiah.

Religions of Egypt

Some religions, however, like ancient Egyptian, for example, couldn't complete an imposed transition from primarily polytheistic spiritual beliefs to a monotheistic religion. The Egyptians believed their world was created by the gods, and as such, they could either be in their favor or an object of their wrath. Pharaohs dedicated their reigns to building and commissioning temples to major deities, which changed throughout time. They also spent their lives building monumental tombs and employed complex funerary rituals to assure immortality for their souls in the afterlife.

Egyptians believed their pharaohs had divine powers gifted from the gods. Pharaohs even acted as intermediaries between the common people and the gods, and it was believed the gods spoke through the words and deeds of the rulers. Ancient Egyptians had to make offerings and perform rituals for these deities, as they were convinced this was the best way to maintain sacred connections.

Akhenaten tried to convert the Egyptian religion to monotheism with his wife, Nefertiti. They established a religious cult that revolved around worshiping a single god called Aten, who was represented as the sun disc. However, this transformation didn't last long. After several generations, the polytheistic religion was fully revived by one of the greatest rulers of the New Kingdom: Ramesses II.

Popular deities, however, changed from one dynasty to another and even from one pharaoh to the next. The cult of Horus had the strongest presence with the first dynasties. Other popular deities were the god creator Amun, the sun god Ra, the mother goddess Isis, Set, Anubis, Horus, and the monotheistic deity Aten. There were even cults where two gods became one, like Amun-Ra, for instance. Egyptians also believed that the gods could be manifested through animals, so they had animal cults. Many of their deities are represented as half-human, half-animal.

Chapter 11 – Politics and International Relations in the Fertile Crescent

Wars tend to set the weak and the strong apart, and the warrior kings and pharaohs who led their armies into battle were praised as great heroes before and after their death. And they had many opportunities to prove themselves. The empires and kingdoms in the ancient Near East were ravaged by rebellions and civil wars, not to mention the wars they led on each other. The earliest civil war, a battle for the throne, took place in ancient Egypt before the unification of Upper and Lower Egypt around 3000 BCE. The Mesopotamian cities of Lagash, Uruk, and Kish fought for hegemony in the region in 2500 BCE. These conflicts came to an end with the arrival of Lugal-zage-si, who conquered several Sumerian city-states and overthrew rulers of smaller cities. Wars quickly changed the political and geopolitical scene in the ancient Near East, as kingdoms and empires soon began to form.

War wasn't the only option, although there were many throughout the period of the ancient Near East. Peace was also needed for prosperity, and some rulers appeared to be more skilled in diplomacy than in waging wars. However, almost every ruler led war expeditions. This could have been to expand their empire, but wars were also conducted to gain valuable and unique goods from other regions. This would have included exotic items, food, building materials, and ores. Trading and preserving resources were often the main motives behind treaties, as wars emptied the treasuries of kingdoms. By settling on peaceful terms, rulers would be able to conserve their riches and also receive goods that were not indigenous to their region.

There were many important relationships between the kingdoms of the ancient Near East. One such relationship was between Mesopotamia and Egypt. This started in the 4th millennium BCE in the period of Prehistoric Egypt and the Uruk period in Mesopotamia. The two cultures established a trading route and exchanged goods and arts, and the influence of both cultures was visible in Egypt and Mesopotamia. During the Hyksos period, Egypt established a diplomatic relationship with the Hittites and Crete, and later on, the kingdom established a diplomatic relationship with Mitanni as well.

The relationships between the Mesopotamians, Babylonians, and Assyrians greatly varied with the Levant. War, trade, and diplomatic relationships were common throughout the centuries. Parts of the Levant were even subdued by Babylon and Assyria as a part of the expansion of these kingdoms.

Wars were often interweaved with diplomatic relationships and treaties, leading to prosperity and peace in the lands that had been ravaged by battles. However, wars brought prosperity to the victors as well, as they brought back treasures to their kingdoms. Kingdoms and city-states that had been weakened by famine, floods, and other catastrophes were easy prey to imperialistic kingdoms, and at times, such kingdoms were forced to usurp other territories to resolve their problems while utilizing the last of their resources on acquiring solutions. Alliances were formed to repel stronger and mutual enemies, and political marriages were arranged to form stronger relationships between kingdoms and city-states.

The relationships in the ancient Near East were dynamic and greatly depended on the rulers and how they wanted to approach the situation. These relationships were what made the Fertile Crescent the Cradle of Civilization.

Conclusion

All of the mighty empires known to history started as humble settlements that later transformed into something spectacular. They were powerful and influential, but in the end, they experienced turmoil and crumbled. The changing dominance over the banks of powerful rivers in the ancient Near East brought life and prosperity to some, while others suffered. The mighty and the mightier were constantly warring for power and dominance. However, the driving force behind the rise of these civilizations was the fertility of the region.

From nomadic groups to small settlements that formed complex governance to the first city-states, the Fertile Crescent in the ancient Near East witnessed the rise of the first empire. It watched as religions developed for thousands of years, influencing and becoming some of the major religions today. Gods and kings were born, and gods and kings died. However, these gods and kings assured their immortality through the written word. This is what separates the civilizations of the ancient Near East from the many peoples who inhabited the region.

Our knowledge of these times comes from written sources, art, statues, monuments, and religious, ritual, and everyday objects. Just like the countries today, these civilizations waged wars, suffered from droughts and famine, and traded and crossed paths with each other.

Even millennia later, it still feels as if we are walking in the footsteps of those who came before us.

Here's another book by Captivating History that you might be interested in

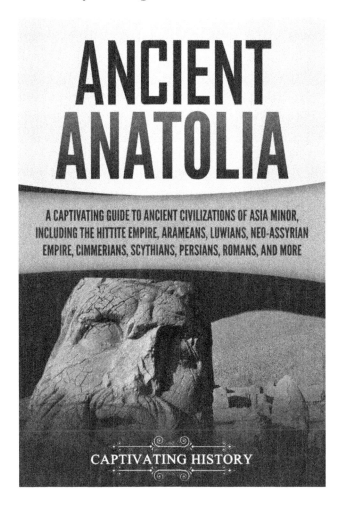

Free Bonus from Captivating History (Available for a Limited time)

Hi History Lovers!

Now you have a chance to join our exclusive history list so you can get your first history ebook for free as well as discounts and a potential to get more history books for free! Simply visit the link below to join.

Captivatinghistory.com/ebook

Also, make sure to follow us on Facebook, Twitter and Youtube by searching for Captivating History.

References

• Gregory D. Mumford, *The Oxford Handbook of the Archaeology of the Levant: c. 8000-332 BCE*, Edited by Ann E. Killebrew and Margreet Steiner

• William W. Hallo & William Kelly Simpson, *The Ancient Near East: A History*, Holt Rinehart and Winston Publishers, 2nd edition, 1997. ISBN 0-15-503819-2.

• Marc Van de Mieroop, *History of the Ancient Near East: Ca. 3000-323 B.C.*, Blackwell Publishers, 2nd edition, 2006 (first published 2003). ISBN 1-4051-4911-6.

• Ergil, Doğu, PKK: The Kurdistan Workers' Party, in Marianne Heiberg, Brendan O'Leary, John Tirman, eds., *Terror, Insurgency, and the State: Ending Protracted Conflicts*, University of Pennsylvania Press, 2007.

• Liverani, M., *International Relations in the Ancient Near East*, 2001. Palgrave Macmillan UK, ISBN. 978-0-230-28639-9.

• *Cultural Atlas of Mesopotamia and the Ancient Near East*, An Andromeda book, An Equinox book, Armenian Research Center collection, Facts on File, 1990, ISBN 0816022186, 9780816022182

- Jack M. Sasson, John Baines, Gary Beckman, Karen S. Rubinson, *Civilizations of the Ancient Near East,* Book 1, Scribner, 1995.

- William H. Stiebing Jr., Susan N. Helft, *Ancient Near Eastern History and Culture,* Taylor & Francis, 2017, ISBN 1134880839, 9781134880836

- Daniel C. Snell, *Life in the Ancient Near East, 3100-332 B.C.E. New Edition,* ISBN-13: 978-0300076660, ISBN-10: 0300076665

- Louis Lawrence Orlin, *Life and Thought in the Ancient Near East,* University of Michigan Press, 2007, ISBN-10: 0472069926, ISBN-13: 978-0472069927

- Donald B. Redford, *Egypt, Canaan, and Israel in Ancient Times,* Princeton University Press; New Ed edition, 1993, ISBN-10: 0691000867, ISBN-13: 978-0691000862

- Mark Van De Mieroop, *The Eastern Mediterranean in the Age of Ramesses II,* ISBN:9781405160698, ISBN:9780470696644

- Pierre-Louis Gatier, Robert-Louis Gatier, Eric Gubel, Philippe *The Levant: History and Archaeology in the Eastern Mediterranean,* Konemann, 2000, ISBN-10: 3829004958, ISBN-13: 978-3829004954.

- Nicolas Grimal, Ian Shaw (translator): *A History of Ancient Egypt,* 1992, Oxford: Blackwell Publishing, ISBN 978-0-63-119396-8.

- Michael Rice: *Egypt's Making: The Origins of Ancient Egypt, 5000-2000 BC.* Taylor & Francis, London/New York 1990, ISBN 0-415-05092-8.

- Luckenbill, Daniel David (1927). *Ancient Records of Assyria and Babylonia.* Ancient records. 2: Historical records of Assyria: from Sargon to the end. Chicago: The University of Chicago Press. *Retrieved 3 February 2019.*

- Arnold, Bill T. *(2005). Who Were the Babylonians?* Brill Publishers. ISBN 978-90-04-13071-5.

- DeBlois, Lukas *(1997). An Introduction to the Ancient World. Routledge.* ISBN 978-0-415-12773-8.

- Van De Mieroop, Marc *(2005). King Hammurabi of Babylon: A Biography.* Blackwell Publishing. ISBN 978-1-4051-2660-1.

- Liverani, Mario. *Imagining Babylon: The Modern Story of an Ancient City.* Translated from Italian to English by Ailsa Campbell. Boston: De Gruyter, 2016. ISBN 978-1-61451-602-6.

- Seymour, M. J. *(2006). The Idea of Babylon: Archaeology and Representation in Mesopotamia (Doctoral thesis).* University College London. OCLC 500097655

- D. T. Potts, *The Archaeology of Elam: Formation and Transformation of an Ancient Iranian State.* Cambridge World Archaeology. Cambridge University Press, 2015 ISBN 1107094690

- Bierbrier, M. L. *The Late New Kingdom in Egypt, C. 1300-664 B.C.: A Genealogical and Chronological Investigation.* Warminster, England: Aris & Phillips, 1975.

- Thomas, Angela P. *Akhenaten's Egypt.* Shire Egyptology 10. Princes Risborough, UK: The Shire, 1988.

- Morkot, Robert. *A Short History of New Kingdom Egypt.* London: Tauris, 2015.

9 781647 489762

Printed by BoD™in Norderstedt, Germany